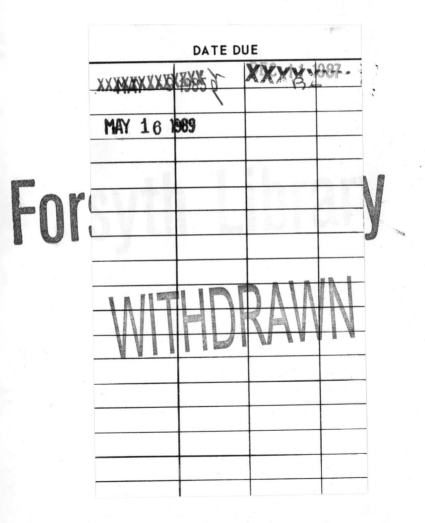

Legal Almanac Series No. 79

CHILD ABUSE:
Governing Law & Legislation

Irving J. Sloan, J.D.
Editor and Compiler

1983
OCEANA PUBLICATIONS, INC.
London • Rome • New York

This is the seventy-ninth number in a series of LEGAL ALMANACS which bring you the law on various subjects in nontechnical language. These books do not take the place of your attorney's advice, but they can introduce you to your legal rights and responsibilities.

Library of Congress Cataloging in Publication Data

Sloan, Irving J.
  Child abuse.

  1. Child abuse—Law and legislation—United
States. I. Title.
KF9323.S57   344.73'037044   82-22293
ISBN 0-379-11142-X 347.30437044   AACR2

Manufactured in the United States of America

TABLE OF CONTENTS

ACKNOWLEDGMENT

The materials presented in this volume have been edited and compiled from publications produced by grants awarded by the National Center on Child Abuse and Neglect; Children's Bureau, Administration for Children, Youth and Families; Office of Human Development; U.S. Department of Health and Human Services, Washington, D.C.

Chapter 1
RECOGNIZING CHILD ABUSE AND NEGLECT*

Child abuse and neglect is usually divided into four major types: physical abuse, neglect, sexual abuse, and emotional maltreatment. Each has recognizable characteristics. More often than not, a particular type of child abuse or neglect can be identified by recognizing physical and behavioral indicators in the child, and clues in the parents' attitudes and behaviors.

Physical indicators of child abuse and neglect are indicators which usually are readily observable. They may be mild or severe, but they involve the child's physical appearance. Frequently, they include skin or bone injuries, or lack of care manifested in such conditions as malnutrition. The child's behavior can sometimes be a clue to the presence of child abuse or neglect. Behavioral indicators may exist alone, or in combination with physical indicators. They may be subtle or they may be graphic statements by the child. For the adolescent particularly, behavior may be the only clue of abuse or neglect. Child abuse or neglect occurs among children of all ages. It is estimated that half of child abuse and neglect children are over five years of age, and a growing number are adolescents.

INDICATORS IN THE CHILD

Physical Abuse

Physical abuse of children includes any non-accidental parental injury caused by the child's

*Source: The Role of Law Enforcement in the Prevention and Treatment of Child Abuse and Neglect, developed by D.D. Broadhurst and J.S. Knoeller, edited by Kirschner Associates, Inc., for the National Center on Child Abuse and Neglect, U.S. Department of Health and Human Services, Washington, D.C. (1979)

1

caretaker. It may include burning, beating, branding, punching and so on. By definition the injury is not an accident, but neither is it necessary to find that the child's caretaker intended to injure the child. Physical abuse may result from over-discipline or from punishment which is inappropriate to the child's age or condition.

Physical Indicators of Physical Abuse

The following are physical indicators of physical abuse in the school-age child:

Unexplained bruises and welts

- on the face, lips, or mouth

- in various stages of healing (bruises of different colors, for example, or old and new scars together)

- on large areas of the torso, back, buttocks or thighs

- in clusters, forming regular patterns, or reflective of the article used to inflict them (electrical cords, belt buckles)

Unexplained burns

- cigar or cigarette burns, especially on the soles of the feet, palms of the hands, back or buttocks or genitalia

- immersion or "wet" burns, including glove- or sock-like burns and doughnut-shaped burns on the buttocks or genitalia

---

under Contract No. HEW-105-77-1050.

- patterned or "dry" burns which
  show a clearly defined mark left
  by the instrument used to inflict
  them (e.g. electrical burner;
  iron)

- rope burns on the arms, legs,
  neck or torso

Unexplained fractures

- to the skull, nose or facial
  structure

- in various stages of healing
  (indicating they occurred at
  different times)

- multiple or spiral fractures

- swollen or tender limbs

- any fracture in a child under the
  age of two

Unexplained lacerations and abrasions

- to the mouth, lips, gums or eyes

- to the external genitalia

- on the backs of the arms, legs,
  or torso

Unexplained abdominal injuries

- swelling of the abdomen

- localized tenderness

- constant vomiting

Human bite marks, especially when they
appear adult size or are recurrent.

Behavioral Indicators of Physical Abuse

Conduct, too, can be a tip-off to the presence of child abuse and neglect. Abused and neglected children may demonstrate certain characteristic behavior or conduct which can be spotted by the sensitive professional as well as by the layman. For the adolescent particularly, behavior may be the only clue to child abuse and neglect. These behaviors may exist independent of or in conjunction with physical indicators.

The following are some of the behaviors which may be associated with physical abuse:

- is wary of physical contact with adults (The abused child will often avoid it, sometimes even shrinking at the touch or approach of an adult)

- becomes apprehensive when other children cry

- demonstrates extremes in behavior-- extreme aggressiveness or extreme withdrawal, for example-- behavior which lies outside the range expected for the child's age group

- seems frightened of the parents

- states he/she is afraid to go home, or cries when it is time to leave

- reports injury by a parent

Neglect

Neglect involves inattention to the basic needs of a child, such as food, clothing, shelter, medical care, and supervision. While physical abuse tends to be episodic, neglect tends to be chronic. When considering the possibility of neglect, it is important to note the consistency of indicators. Do they occur rarely, or frequently? Are they chronic (there most of the time), period-

4

ic (noticeable after week-ends or absences), or episodic (see twice in a time when there was illness in the family)? In a given community or sub-population, do all the children display these indicators, or only a few? Is this culturally acceptable childrearing, a different lifestyle, or true neglect? Answers to questions like these can be extremely helpful in differentiating between neglect and differing ways of life.

Physical Indicators of Neglect

The following are physical indicators of neglect:

- constant hunger, poor hygiene, or inappropriate clothing

- consistent lack of supervision, especially when engaged in dangerous activities over extended periods of time

- constant fatigue or listlessness

- unattended physical problems or medical needs, such as untreated or infected wounds

Behavioral Indicators of Neglect

The following behaviors are significant enough to consider the existence of neglect:

- begging or stealing food

- constantly falling asleep in class

- rare attendance at school

- coming to school very early and leaving very late

- addiction to alcohol or other drugs

- engaging in delinquent acts such as

vandalism or theft

- stating that there is no one to
  care or look after him/her.

Sexual Abuse

Sexual abuse includes any contacts or interactions between a child and an adult in which the
child is being used for the sexual stimulation of
the perpetrator or another person. These acts,
when committed by a person under the age of 18
who is either significantly older than the victim
or in a position of power or control over another
child, may be considered sexual abuse.

PHYSICAL INDICATORS OF

SEXUAL ABUSE

Sexual abuse is not often identified through
physical indicators alone. Frequently a child con-
fides in a trusted teacher or counselor or nurse
that he or she has been sexually assaulted or
molested by a caretaker, and that may be the first
sign that sexual abuse is occurring.

There are some physical signs to be alert
for, however. These include:

- difficulty in walking or sitting

- torn, stained, or bloody underclothing

- complaints of pain or itching in
  the genital area

- bruises or bleeding in external
  genitalia, vaginal or anal area

- veneral disease, particularly in
  a child under 13

- pregnancy, especially in early
  adolescence.

The sexually abused child may:

- appear withdrawn; engage in
  fantasy or infantile behavior;
  even appear retarded

- have poor peer relationships

- be unwilling to change for gym
  or to participate in physical
  activities

- engage in delinquent acts, or
  run away

- display bizarre, sophisticated,
  or unusual sexual knowledge or
  behavior

- state he/she has been sexually
  assaulted by a caretaker.

Emotional Maltreatment

Emotional maltreatment includes blaming,
belittling or rejecting a child; constantly
treating siblings unequally; and persistent lack
of concern by the caretaker for the child's welfare. Emotional maltreatment is rarely manifest
in physical signs; speech disorders, lags in
physical development, and failure-to-thrive syndrome (which is a progressive wasting away usually associated with lack of mothering) are a few
physical indicators of emotional maltreatment.
More often it is observed through behavioral indicators, and even these indicators may not be
immediately apparent.

Behavioral Indicators of Emotional Maltreatment

While emotional maltreatment does occur
alone, it often accompanies physical abuse and
sometimes sexual abuse. Emotionally maltreated
children are not always physically abused, but
physically abused children are almost always
emotionally maltreated as well. The emotionally
maltreated child may demonstrate the following

behavioral characteristics:[1]

- <u>habit disorders</u> such as sucking, biting, rocking, enuresis, or feeding disorders

- <u>conduct disorders</u> including withdrawal and anti-social behavior such as destructiveness, cruelty and stealing

- <u>neurotic traits</u> such as sleep disorders and inhibition of play

- <u>psychoneurotic reactions</u> including hysteria, obsession, compulsion, phobias and hypochondria

- <u>behavior extremes</u> such as appearing overly compliant, extremely passive or aggressive, very demanding or undemanding

- <u>overly adaptive behaviors</u> which are either inappropriately adult (parenting other children, for example) or inappropriately infantile (rocking, head-banging or thumbsucking, for example)

- <u>lags</u> in emotional and intellectual development

- <u>attempted suicide</u>

The behavior of emotionally maltreated and emotionally disturbed children is similar. However, parental behavior can help to distinguish disturbance from maltreatment. The parents of an emotionally disturbed child generally accept the existence of a problem. They are concerned about the child's welfare and are actively seeking help. The parents of an emotionally maltreated child

---

[1]<u>Protective Services and Emotional Neglect</u>. Max Wild. Denver: The American Human Association, 1961, pp.6-7.

often blame the child for the problem (or ignore its existence), refuse all offers of help, and are unconcerned about the child's welfare.

INDICATORS IN THE PARENT

The behavior and attitudes of the parents, their own life histories, even the condition of their home, can offer valuable clues to the presence of child abuse and neglect. When considering the possibility of child abuse and neglect, the professional and the layman as well, should evaluate to what extent the parents seem to be: concerned or unconcerned about the child; looking for solutions or denying the existence of a problem; hostile or cooperative.

The following is a list of characteristics based on a composite of many cases. This list is not exhaustive; many more indicators exist than can be included. Neither does the presence of a single or even several indicators <u>prove</u> that maltreatment exists.

Characteristics of Abusive Parents

These parents:

- seem unconcerned about the child

- see the child as "bad," "evil," a "monster" or "witch"

- offer illogical, unconvincing, contradictory explanations or have no explanation of the child's injury

- attempt to conceal the child's injury or to protect the identity of person(s) responsible

- routinely employ harsh, unreasonable discipline which is inappropriate to child's age, transgressions, and condition

- were often abused as children

- were expected to meet high demands
  of their parents

- were unable to depend on their
  parents for love and nurturance

- cannot provide emotionally for
  themselves as adults

- expect their children to fill
  their emotional void

- have poor impulse control

- expect rejection

- have low self-esteem

- are emotionally immature

- are isolated, have no support
  system

- marry a spouse who is not emotionally
  supportive and who passively supports
  the abuse.

Characteristics of Neglectful Parents

These parents:

- may have a chaotic home life

- may live in unsafe conditions
  (no food; garbage and excrement
  in living areas; exposed wiring;
  drugs and poisons kept within
  the reach of children)

- may abuse drugs or alcohol

- may be mentally retarded, have

low I.Q., or have a flat person-
ality

- may be impulsive individuals who
  seek immediate gratification without regard to long-term consequences

- may be motivated and employed but
  unable to find or afford child
  care

- generally have not experienced
  success

- had emotional needs which are not
  met by their parents

- have low self-esteem

- have little motivation or skill
  to effect changes in their lives

- tend to be passive

Characteristics of Sexually Abusive Parents

The most typical type of reported intra-
familial sexual abuse occurs between an adult
male, either the father or the mother's sexual
partner, and a female child living in the same
house.

These parents:

- have low self-esteem

- had emotional needs which were
  not met by their parents

- have inadequate coping skills

- may have experienced the loss of
  their spouse through death or
  divorce

- may be experiencing over-crowding

11

in their home

- may have marital problems
  causing one spouse to seek
  physical affection from a
  child rather than the other
  spouse (a situation the "denying"
  husband or wife might find acceptable)

- may abuse alcohol

- lack social and emotional
  contacts outside the family

- have cultural standards which
  determine the degree of acceptable body contact.

The adult male:

- is often a rigid disciplinarian

- is passive outside the home

- does not usually have a police
  record nor is he known to be
  involved in any public disturbance

- does not engage in social activities
  outside the home

- is jealous and protective of the
  child

- often initiates sexual contact with
  the child by hugging and kissing
  which tends to develop over time
  into more caressing, genital-genital
  and oral-genital contacts.

The mother:

- is frequently cognizant of the sexual
  abuse but subconsciously denies it

- may hesitate reporting for fear of
  destroying the marriage and being
  left on her own

- may see sexual activity within the
  family as preferable to extra-marital
  affairs

- may feel that the sexual activity
  between the husband and daughter
  is a relief from her wifely sexual
  responsibilities and will make
  certain that time is available for
  the two to be alone

- often feels a mixture of guilt and
  jealousy toward her daughter.

Chapter 2

REPORTING CHILD ABUSE AND NEGLECT: STATE LAWS*

Introduction

The enactment of child abuse and neglect reporting laws by state legislatures began in earnest in the early 1960's. It coincided with the first formalized medical profile of the abused or battered child and increasing community awareness of the extent of the problem. Workers dealing with families in crisis had become concerned not only with identification of the problem but also with treatment and prevention of the underlying causes and sought legislation to aid their efforts.

The idea of a child abuse reporting statute was first explored in 1962, and in 1963 a model reporting statute was proposed by the Children's Bureau of the then HEW. By 1965, two other models had been developed and were offered to the public. Reporting statutes were enacted in 20 states by 1964 and in 49 states by 1966. Today all 50 states, the District of Columbia, American Samoa, Guam, Puerto Rico, and the Virgin Islands have reporting laws.

This chapter surveys key elements of the statutes dealing with the reporting of suspected or known cases of child abuse and neglect. These are: the purpose of the state reporting laws, reportable circumstances, the definition of abuse and neglect, age limits of children, the required state of mind of the reporter, and who must and may report. Also discussed are immunity for re-

---

*Source: Child Abuse & Neglect, State Reporting Laws, Developed by Herner and Company for the National Center on Child Abuse and Neglect, U.S. Department of Health and Human Services (1980).

porting and other acts, abrogation of privileges, special exemptions, and the criminal and civil sanctions imposed for failure to report.

Purpose Clause

Forty-three jurisdictions now explicitly state a purpose in their reporting laws. Almost all purpose clauses emphasize the protection of children.

> ... to protect children whose health or welfare may be jeopardized through physical abuse, neglect or sexual abuse; to strengthen the family and make the home safe for children through improvement of parental and guardian capacity for responsible child care; and to provide a safe temporary or permanent home environment for physically or sexually abused children; to provide for the voluntary reporting of abuse or neglect of children; to require the investigation of such reporting; and to provide protective and counseling services in appropriate cases.

> -MINN. STAT. ANN. §626 556(1) (SUPP. 1981)

> ... to provide for the protection of children under 18 years of age who have had serious injury inflicted upon them by other than accidental means. It is the intent of this legislation to assure that the lives of innocent children are immediately safeguarded from further injury and possible death and that the legal rights

of such children are fully protected.

-N.J. STAT. ANN. §9:6-8.8
(SUPP. 1981)

The purpose of any reporting statute is three-fold: first, to identify the child in peril as quickly as possible; second, to designate an agency to receive and investigate reports of suspected child abuse; and third, to offer, where appropriate, services and treatment. The purpose clause in most jurisdictions' reporting statutes includes a provision that encourages increased reporting of suspected cases of abuse and neglect, which is the first step in providing the greatest possible protection for children whose health and welfare may be adversely affected. Many purpose clauses also state that protective services will be provided to prevent further abuse. A majority of states also declare that the purpose of state intervention will be to preserve the unity and welfare of the family whenever possible, with services provided within the family environment.

Purpose clauses also are found in statutory provisions authorizing judicial proceedings. The purpose often stated is to provide judicial procedures in which the parties are assured a fair hearing and their constitutional and other legal rights are recognized and enforced. Another stated purpose is to separate clearly in the judicial process the abused or neglected child from the delinquent child and to provide appropriate and distinct options for the disposition and treatment of these children.

Reportable Circumstances

What circumstances or conditions must or may be reported? Every jurisdiction requires that suspected cases of child abuse be reported. Over the years states have broadened the concept of reportable circumstances by either expanding the definition of child abuse to include physical injury, emotional harm, sexual abuse and exploitation, and neglect, or by expressly requiring circumstances in addition to child abuse to be reported. It should be noted that the reporting law of 48 jurisdictions specifically include neglect as a reportable condition.

All state and territory laws are similar to the Model Child Protection Act in that they do not require a reporter to know or to be certain that a child has been abused or neglected. The degree of certainty most often expressed is "reason to believe" or "reasonable cause to believe or suspect," a standard based on the reasonable person's convictions. A few jurisdictions also require reports when one "observes the child being subjected to conditions or circumstances which would reasonably result in child abuse or neglect." For example, Arkansas, Colorado, Idaho, Maine, Utah, West Virginia, American Samoa, and the Virgin Islands, require such reports.

> ...any wound, injury, disability, or physical or mental condition which is of such a nature as to reasonably indicate that it has been caused by brutality, abuse or neglect or which on the basis of available information reasonably appears to have been caused by brutality, abuse or neglect...

> -TENN. CODE ANN. §37-1230 (SUPP. 1980)

Definitions of Child Abuse and Neglect

Each jurisdiction defines child abuse and neglect differently, and many jurisdictions have more than one definition. These definitions are found not only in reporting laws but also in juvenile court laws, criminal codes, and welfare laws. Some jurisdictions define child abuse and neglect as a single concept; other jurisdictions have separate definitions for child abuse and child neglect. Statutory definitions of child abuse and neglect and distinctions between abuse

18

and neglect are among the most unsettled and controversial issues in the child protection area. One view of the controversy involving these definitions is found in the Model Child Protection commentary:

> The time and effort spent in trying to distinguish between abuse and neglect serves no useful purpose. Differentiating between abuse and neglect neither establishes nor justifies service priorities; it only confuses the definition of what is reportable, thereby hindering accurate reporting, and detracting from the individualized handling of cases. A child may suffer serious or permanent harm and even death as a result of neglect. Therefore, the same reasons that justify the mandatory reporting of abuse require the mandatory reporting of child neglect.
>
> - MODEL ACT, p.17

A survey of the definitions reveals a broad list of maltreatment that constitutes abuse and neglect, including battering; dependency, deprivation; abandonment; exploitation, over-work; emotional maltreatment; failure to provide necessities, proper supervision, or care; and excessive corporal punishment.

One common generalized expression of reportable maltreatment that appears in many statutes is "harm or threatened harm to a child's welfare by the acts of omissions of his/her parent or other person responsible for his/her welfare," which follows the language in the Model Act definition of "abuse or neglect." The term "harm or threatened harm" is usually further defined in the statutes. A typical definition of neglect is "a failure to provide, by those legally responsible for the care of the child, the proper or necessary support, education as required by law, or medical, surgical, or any other care necessary for his well-being." Abuse is often defined as "any physical injury, sexual abuse or mental injury inflicted on a child other than by accidental means by a person responsible for the child's health or welfare." Several states specify a variety of specific manifestations of abuse, such as "skin bruising, bleeding, malnutrition, failure to thrive, burns, fractures of any bone, subdural hematoma or soft tissue swelling."

Over the years many states have broadened the concept of reportable abuse to include sexual abuse and exploitation and mental or emotional injury. A growing number of jurisdictions also have specifically defined these terms. For example, almost all jurisdictions now include sexual abuse in their definition of child abuse. Maryland has defined sexual abuse in its reporting law as:

> ...any act or acts involving molestation or exploitation, including but not limited to incest, rape, or sexual offense in any degree, sodomy or unnatural or perverted sexual practices on a child...

> - MD. CODE ANN. Art. 27,
> §35A(b) (8) (SUPP. 1978)

Florida has broadened its definition of abuse to include sexual exploitation:

> "Abuse" or "maltreatment" also includes the aiding, abetting, counseling, hiring, or procuring of a child to perform or participate in any photograph, motion picture, exhibition, show, representation, or other presentation which, in whole or in part, depicts sexual con-

20

duct, sexual excitement, or
sadomasochistic abuse involving a child.

-FLA, STAT. ANN. §827.07(1)(b)

Over half of the jurisdictions include the
element of mental or emotional injury in their
definitions of child abuse. Wyoming defines mental injury as:

...an injury to the psychological
capacity or emotional stability
of a child as evidenced by an observable or substantial impairment in his/her ability to function within a normal range of
performance and behavior with
due regard to his/her culture...

-WYO. STAT. §14-3-202(a)(ii)

Corporal punishment can be defined as non-
accidental physical injury, and, as such, it
would seem to fall within the typical statutory
definition of child abuse. No state, however,
prohibits parents from using reasonable corporal
punishment in the upbringing of their children.
Five jurisdictions expressly permit the use of
reasonable corporal punishment and note that it
is not child abuse: Colorado, Ohio, Oklahoma,
South Carolina, and Washington.

In addition, 26 jurisdictions provide for
the justified use of force upon a minor person
responsible for his/her care and supervision to
the extent reasonably necessary to maintain discipline or to promote the welfare of the minor:
Albama, Arizona, Arkansas, Colorado, Connecticut,
Delaware, Georgia, Hawaii, Kentucky, Louisiana,
Maine, Minnesota, Missouri, Montana, Nebraska,
New Hampshire, New Jersey, New York, North Dakota, Texas, Utah, Washington, and Wisconsin.

These justification statutes do not excuse

or lessen the duty to report child abuse, and
since they only justify the use of reasonable
force, they necessarily preclude a judicial finding of child abuse in cases brought under the
child protection laws.

Age Limits of Reportable Children

The federal Child Abuse Prevention and
Treatment Act defines a child as a person under
the age of 18 or the age specified by the child
protection law of a state (P.L. No. 93-247), as
amended by Act of 1978 (P.L. No. 95-266). Fifty-
four jurisdictions set the age limit of reportable
children at 18 years or younger. Wyoming sets the
reportable age limit at 16.

Several jurisdictions qualify their age limit
or include separate considerations in their laws.
Delaware and American Samoa include mentally retarded persons, regardless of age. Ohio sets the
age at 18 years or any crippled or otherwise physically or mentally handicapped child under 21.
Washington's law applies to adult developmentally
disabled persons, and Nebraska extends protection
to incompetent or disabled persons. Tennessee's
law refers to a person under 18 years or persons
who are reasonably presumed to be under 18 years.
North Dakota's law applies to a person who is
under 18 years and is neither married and co-
habitating with spouse nor in the military service. Texas refers to a person under 18 years who
has not been married or had his/her disabilities
of minority removed for general purposes.

Who Must Report

The earliest focus on mandatory reporting
was directed at physicians. Their training and
contact with injured children singled them out
as the group most likely to detect and report
child abuse and neglect. Table A shows that every
jurisdiction requires physicians to report child
abuse. This is mandated either by specific mention
of physicians or by a more general directive,
such as "practitioners of the healing arts" or

22

"by any person."

A recent survey indicated that only 1.6% of the child abuse reports filed in the United States came from private physicians. Physicians do not have daily access to young children, and, in most cases, a physician only sees a child when the injuries are so severe that they require immediate attention medically. Over the years, jurisdictions have broadened the base of mandated reporters to include persons who have more frequent contact with children. Table A indicates which states require reports from other professionals, such as teachers and law enforcement and child care personnel.

Reports from teachers or other school personnel are specifically mandated by 45 jurisdictions. Forty-six jurisdictions require reports from social service workers. Forty-seven jurisdictions require reports from nurses. Twenty-five states and two territories mandate reports from coroners or medical examiners. Reports from clergymen are required in seven states and attorneys are included in four reporting laws.

Nineteen jurisdictions mandate "any person" or "any other person" to report. In addition, a variety of persons not included in the categories in Table A are required to make reports. Arizona, Louisiana, and Missouri require reports from any "other person with responsibility for the care of children." Florida requires reports from "any person, including, but not limited to...employees of a public or private facility serving children." Pennsylvania's law focuses on "any person who, in the course of their profession comes into contact with children." Alabama mandates reports from "any other person called upon to render aid or medical assistance to any child"; Oregon speaks of "any public or private official." North Dakota, West Virginia, and the Virgin Islands require reports from "any other medical professional." Virginia includes "any person licensed to practice medicine...and any professional staff person employed or state-operated hospital, institution

Table A
WHO REPORTS

WHO MUST REPORT	Alabama	Alaska	Arizona	Arkansas	California	Colorado	Connecticut	Delaware	District of Columbia	Florida	Georgia	Hawaii	Idaho	Illinois	Indiana	Iowa	Kansas	Kentucky	Louisiana	Maine	Maryland	Massachusetts	Michigan	Minnesota	Mississippi	Missouri
CORONER/MEDICAL EXAMINER	×		×	×		×	×	×	×			×	×	×				×		×		×		×	×	×
PRACTITIONER OF HEALING ARTS	×	×	×	×		×	×	×	×		×					×	×	×		×	×			×	×	×
PHARMACIST	×																									
PODIATRIST	×		×		×	×	×			×			×		×			×								×
OPTOMETRIST	×	×				×									×		×									×
CHIROPRACTOR	×	×	×		×	×	×		×				×		×		×		×							×
PRACTITIONER OF HEALING ARTS¹		×					×			×				×	×			×				×		×		×
HOSPITAL/INSTITUTION PERSONNEL	×	×		×	×	×							×		×		×	×					×			×
INTERN			×	×	×	×	×	×		×		×		×	×	×	×	×	×	×				×	×	
RESIDENT			×	×	×		×	×		×		×		×	×	×	×	×	×					×	×	
DENTIST	×	×	×	×	×	×	×	×	×	×		×	×		×		×	×	×		×	×	×	×	×	×
OSTEOPATH	×	×	×	×		×	×	×		×	×		×		×		×		×		×					
SURGEON	×	×	×	×	×	×	×						×		×				×							
NURSE	×	×	×	×	×	×	×	×	×	×	×	×	×	×	×		×	×	×	×	×	×	×	×	×	×
PHYSICIAN	×	×	×	×	×	×	×	×	×	×	×	×	×	×	×		×		×	×	×	×	×	×	×	×
ANY PERSONS							×	×		×			×		×			×	×							

Montana
Nebraska
Nevada
New Hampshire
New Jersey
New Mexico
New York
North Carolina
North Dakota
Ohio
Oklahoma
Oregon
Pennsylvania
Rhode Island
South Carolina
South Dakota
Tennessee
Texas
Utah
Vermont
Virginia
Washington
West Virginia
Wisconsin
Wyoming
America Samoa
Guam
Puerto Rico
Virgin Islands

Numbers refer to footnotes for Tables A through H.

*/ state that does not specify categories of professionals that must report, but instead requires that every person or any person report, is checked only in this column.

25

	Alabama	Alaska	Arizona	Arkansas	California	Colorado	Connecticut	Delaware	District of Columbia	Florida	Georgia	Hawaii	Idaho	Illinois	Indiana	Iowa	Kansas	Kentucky	Louisiana	Maine	Maryland	Massachusetts	Michigan	Minnesota	Mississippi	Missouri
Permissive Reporting	●	●		●	●	●			●		●	●		●		●	●	●	●		●	●	●			●
Others 4	×	×	×		×	×				×				×			×	×			×	×	×			×
Attorney																										
Clergyman					×		×																		×	×
Child Care Institution/Worker	×			×	×	×	×		×		×		×	×		×		×		×			×	×	×	×
Religious Healing Practitioner 3		×			×	×								×						×						×
Parole Officer																							×			×
Probation Officer					×																		×	×		×
Police Officers							×																×	×		
Peace Officer	×	×	×	×	×	×										×		×								×
Law Enforcement Officer	×			×				×	×		×			×			×		×	×			×	×	×	×
Social Services Worker	×	×	×	×	×	×	×	×	×	×	×	×	×	×	×	×	×	×	×	×	×	×	×	×	×	×
Other School Personnel	×			×	×	×	×	×	×	×		×		×		×	×	×		×	×	×	×	×	×	×
Teachers 2	×	×	×	×	×	×	×	×	×	×	×	×	×	×	×			×	×	×	×	×	×	×	×	×

Row group labels: "WHO MAY REPORT" (top), "WHO MUST REPORT" (lower rows). Column block header: "States and Territories".

State	•	1	2	3	4	5	6	7	8	9	10	11	12	13
Montana			X							X	X	X	X	
Nebraska											X	X	X	
Nevada	•		X	X	X					X	X	X	X	
New Hampshire		X	X	X	X					X	X	X	X	
New Jersey														
New Mexico									X		X	X	X	
New York	•				X					X	X	X	X	X
North Carolina		X			X					X	X	X		
North Dakota	•	X			X					X	X	X	X	
Ohio	•	X	X		X					X	X	X	X	
Oklahoma			X											
Oregon		X	X		X	X			X	X	X	X	X	
Pennsylvania	•	X			X	X			X	X	X	X	X	
Rhode Island														
South Carolina					X	X		X		X	X	X	X	
South Dakota	•									X	X			
Tennessee														
Texas														
Utah							X							
Vermont	•	X			X	X				X	X	X	X	
Virginia	•	X			X	X			X	X	X	X	X	
Washington	•	X			X	X		X		X	X	X	X	
West Virginia	•	X			X				X	X	X	X	X	
Wisconsin					X						X	X	X	
Wyoming														
America Samoa					X	X			X	X	X	X	X	
Guam	•		X		X	X			X	X	X	X	X	
Puerto Rico					X						X	X	X	
Virgin Islands	•	X			X			X		X	X	X	X	

or facility which children have been committed to or placed in for care or treatment." California requires reports from "every person, firm, or corporation conducting any hospital in the state or the managing agent thereof; or the person managing or in charge of such hospital, cr in charge of any ward or part of such hospital, who receives a patient from a health care facility..."

One clause, which commonly appears in the reporting laws, requires medical staff to notify the person in charge of the institution, who, in turn, is responsible for the report. This requirement follows the language in Section 5(b) of the 1977 Model Act draft and is aimed at increasing administrative accountability and the establishment of reporting and follow-up procedures. The Arkansas statute, a typical example, reads:

> Whenever such person is required to report... in his capacity as a member of the staff of a medical or public or private institution, school, facility or other agency, he shall immediately notify the person in charge... or his designated agent, who shall then become responsible for making a report or cause such report to be made.
>
> -ARK. STAT. ANN. §42-808

The New York statute does not completely shift the responsibility for reporting once a staff member notifies his superior:

> Whenever such person is required to report under this title in his capacity as a member of the staff of a medical or other public or private institution, school, facility, or agency, he shall immediately notify the person in charge of such institution, school, facility,

or agency, or his designated agent, who then also
shall become responsible to
report or cause reports to
be made. However, nothing
in this section or title
is intended to require more
than one report from any
such institution, school
or agency.

-N.Y. SOC. SERV. LAW §413

Another special clause which appears in many
state laws requires that child fatalities due to
abuse and neglect be reported to medical examiners or coroners and district attorneys. Among the
states so requiring are: Arkansas, Maine, Massachusetts, Minnesota, Missouri, New York, Pennsylvania, Virginia, Washington, West Virginia, and
American Samoa among the territories.

The West Virginia law, which closely follows
the language in section 7 of the Model Act, reads:

Any person or official who is
required...to report cases of
suspected child abuse or neglect
and who has reasonable cause to
suspect that a child has died
as a result of child abuse or
neglect, shall report that fact
to the appropriate medical examiner or coroner. Upon the receipt of such a report, the medical examiner or coroner shall
cause an investigation to be
made and report his findings
to the police, the appropriate
prosecuting attorney, the local
child protective service agency
and, if the institution making
a report is a hospital, to the
hospital.

-W. VA. CODE §49-6A-3
(SUPP. 1978)

Discretion Not to Report

Two states give mandatory reporters discretion not to make a report under certain circumstances. The Maryland child neglect reporting law provides:

> A person required to notify and report under the provisions of this section, need not comply with the notification and reporting requirements of this section if: (1) Efforts are made or will be made to alleviate the conditions which may cause the child to be considered a neglected child and it is concluded by the health practitioner, educator, social worker, or law enforcement officer or agency that these efforts will alleviate these conditions or circumstances; or: (2) The health practitioner, educator, social worker, or law enforcement officer or agency believes that the notification and reporting would inhibit the child, parent, guardian, or custodian from seeking assistance in the future and thereby be detrimental to the child's welfare.
>
> — MD. CODE ANN. Art. 72A (6)(c)

The Maine reporting law states:

> This subsection does not require any person to report when the factual bases for knowing or suspecting child abuse or neglect came from treatment of the individual for suspected child abuse or

neglect, and, in the opinion
of the person required to report, the child's life or health
is not immediately threatened.

                    -ME. REV. STAT. Tit. 22
                    §3853(1)

Who May Report

The last column in Table A shows the 32
jurisdictions which currently provide specific
authorization for permissive reporting. Many
states make no provision for permissive reporting
because they mandate reporting by everyone.

Immunity for Participation in the Making of a Report

One of the eligibility criteria for state
grants under the federal Child Abuse Prevention
Treatment Act is a provision extending "immunity
for persons reporting instances of child abuse
and neglect from prosecution, under any state or
local law, arising out of such reporting." P.L.
No. 93-247, Section 4(b)(2)(A). This provision
encourages full reporting by removing the threat
of legal action from reporters and, in particular,
from medical professionals.

Table B shows that all 50 states, the District of Columbia, American Samoa, Guam, Puerto
Rico, and the Virgin Islands grant immunity from
any liability, civil or criminal, for the making
of a report. This chart also reflects the fact
that most jurisdictions provide additional immunity
for participation in any judicial proceeding resulting from the report.

            (A) No child-care custodian,
            medical practitioner report-
            ing a suspected instance of
            child abuse shall be civilly
            or criminally liable for any
            report required or authorized

31

Table B
IMMUNITY

States and Territories	Good Faith Presumed	Requirement of Good Faith	Immunity in Resulting Judicial Proceedings	Immunity for the Taking of X-rays	Immunity for the Taking of Photographs	Civil and Criminal Immunity in Making of a Report
Alabama			×			×
Alaska		×	×			×
Arizona		×	×		×	×
Arkansas	×					×
California		×	×	×	×	×
Colorado	×		×			×
Connecticut		×	×			×
Delaware		×	×			×
District of Columbia	×	×	×			×
Florida	×		×	×	×	×
Georgia		×	×			×
Hawaii		×	×			×
Idaho		×	×			×
Illinois	×	×	×	×	×	×
Indiana	×	×	×	×	×	×
Iowa		×	×			×
Kansas			×			×
Kentucky		×	×			×
Louisiana			×			×
Maine	×	×	×			×
Maryland		×	×			×
Massachusetts						×
Michigan	×			×¹	×¹	×
Minnesota		×				×
Mississippi	×		×			×
Missouri		×	×	×	×	×
Montana	×		×			×

State						
Nebraska	X				X	
Nevada	X			X	X	
New Hampshire	X			X	X	
New Jersey	X			X	X	
New Mexico	X	X			X	X
New York	X				X	X
North Carolina	X			X	X	
North Dakota	X			X	X	X
Ohio	X			X	X	
Oklahoma	X			X	X	
Oregon	X	X		X	X	X
Pennsylvania	X			X	X	X
Rhode Island	X			X	X	X
South Carolina	X			X	X	X
South Dakota	X			X	X	
Tennessee	X				X	X
Texas	X	X	X			
Utah	X	X	X		X	
Vermont	X			X	X	
Virginia	X			X	X	
Washington	X			X	X	
West Virginia	X[2]	X[2]			X	X
Wisconsin	X[3]	X[3]		X	X	X
Wyoming	X			X	X	X
America Samoa	X	X		X	X	X
Guam	X	X		X	X	X
Puerto Rico	X			X	X	
Virgin Islands	X[4]	X[4]			X	

Numbers refer to footnotes for Tables A through H.

by this article. Any other person reporting a suspected instance of any report authorized by this section unless it
can be proved that a false report was made and the person
knew or should have known that
the report was false. No person
required to make a report pursuant to this section, nor any
person taking photographs at
his or her direction, shall in-
cur any civil or criminal liability for taking photographs
of a suspected victim of child
abuse, without parental consent,
or for disseminating such photographs with the reports required
by this section. However, the
provisions of this section shall
not be construed to grant immunity from such liability with
respect to any other use of such
photographs.

-CAL. PENAL CODE §11172(A)
(WEST 1980)

Anyone participating in good
faith in the making of a report...shall have immunity
from any liability, civil or
criminal, that might otherwise
be incurred or imposed. Any
such participant shall have
the same immunity with respect
to participation in any judicial proceeding resulting
from such report.

-CAL. WELF. & INST. CODE
§16509 (WEST 1980)

Table B also indicates that the majority of
jurisdictions qualify their grant of immunity
with the requirement that the report be made in

good faith. Twenty of these jurisdictions, however, include a presumption of the good faith of reporters. Arizona, Indiana, Louisiana, and North Dakota specifically withhold immunity from reporters if they are charged with or suspected of abusing or neglecting a child who is the subject of a report.

Immunity for the Retention or Removal of a Child

At least 17 jurisdictions explicitly extend the grant of immunity to any person participating in the temporary removal of a child pursuant to state law: Alabama, Arkansas, Colorado, Florida, Illinois, Michigan, Missouri, New Jersey, New York, Pennsylvania, Utah, Virginia, Washington, Wyoming, American Samoa, Guam, and the Virgin Islands.

Immunity for the Taking of Photographs and/or X-rays

Table C indicates that at least 26 jurisdictions specifically authorize some persons or any person to take, or cause to be taken, photographs or X-rays of injury to a child without parental permission. Fifteen of these 26 jurisdictions are those which also specifically grant immunity for the taking of photographs. Ten of the 26 jurisdictions that authorize the taking of photographs or X-rays extend this authorization to any person required to report: Arkansas, Iowa, New York, Ohio, Pennsylvania, South Carolina, West Virginia, American Samoa, Guam, and the Virgin Islands.

The other jurisdictions extend the authorization to physicians or other medical personnel, law enforcement or other social services personnel, or to any person responsible for the child abuse or neglect investigation.

Table C also indicates that 16 jurisdictions require the person authorized to take photographs and/or X-rays to notify the appropriate child protection service of their action or to forward any

Table C
AUTHORITY TO TAKE X-RAYS AND PHOTOGRAPHS

States and Territories	Photographs	X-Rays	Notify of or forward to Child Protective Service	Taken at Public Expense
Alabama				
Alaska				
Arizona	×	×	×	×
Arkansas	×	×		
California	×	×	×	
Colorado				
Connecticut				
Delaware				
District of Columbia	×	×		×
Florida	×	×	×	×
Georgia				
Hawaii				
Idaho				
Illinois	×	×	×	×
Indiana	×	×	×	×
Iowa	×	×		×
Kansas				
Kentucky	×	×		
Louisiana				
Maine				
Maryland				
Massachusetts				
Michigan	×	×	×	
Minnesota				
Mississippi				
Missouri	×	×	×	×

Montana				
Nebraska				
Nevada				
New Hampshire				
New Jersey	X	X	X	
New Mexico				
New York	X	X	X	X
North Carolina				
North Dakota				
Ohio	X	X		
Oklahoma				
Oregon	X			
Pennsylvania	X	X	X	
Rhode Island				
South Carolina	X	X	X	
South Dakota				
Tennessee				
Texas		X		
Utah	X	X	X	
Vermont				
Virginia	X	X		
Washington	X			
West Virginia	X	X	X	X
Wisconsin				
Wyoming	X	X		X
America Samoa	X	X	X	X
Guam	X	X	X	X
Puerto Rico				
Virgin Islands	X	X	X	X

such evidence to that agency.

To encourage complete reporting and the pres-
ervation of evidence of harm, 11 jurisdictions
explicitly authorize that the photographs and X-
rays be taken at public expense.

> Any person or official required
> to report cases of suspected
> child abuse and maltreatment
> may take or cause to be taken
> at public expense photographs
> of the areas of trauma visible
> on a child who is subject to a
> report and, if medically indi-
> cated, cause to be performed
> a radiological examination on
> the child. Any photographs or
> X-rays taken shall be sent to
> the child protective service
> at the time the written report
> is sent, or as soon thereafter
> as possible. Whenever such per-
> son is required to report under
> this title in his capacity as
> a member of the staff of a med-
> ical or other public or private
> institution, school, facility,
> or agency, he shall immediately
> notify the person in charge of
> such institution, school, fa-
> cility, or agency, or his des-
> ignated agent, who shall then
> take or cause to be taken at
> public expense color photographs
> of visible trauma and shall,
> if medically indicated, cause
> to be performed a radiological
> examination on the child.

> -N.Y. SOC. SERV. LAW §416
> (McKINNEY 1976)

Explicit restrictions on the husband-wife
privilege are found in more than 30 jurisdictions.
Another 11 states restrict the husband-wife priv-

ilege by inferences such as exclusion of "all" privileges, "all other privileges except attorney-client," or "any similar privilege" or rule against disclosure.

Four states specifically abrogate the confidential communications privilege for social workers. Six states restrict the minister-penitent communications privilege and five jurisdictions restrict the psychotherapist-patient privilege. Thirteen jurisdictions abrogate the privileges between other professionals, such as counselors and their clients, or waive any privilege provided for by professions or a code of ethics.

> Any privilege between husband and wife, or between any professional person and his client, such as physicians, and ministers, with the exception of attorney and his client, shall not be grounds for excluding evidence at any proceeding regarding the abuse or neglect of the child or the cause thereof.
>
> -LA. REV. STAT. §14:403 (F) (1974)

> In any proceeding resulting from a report... where such report or the contents thereof is sought to be introduced in evidence, such report or contents or any other fact or facts related thereto or to the condition of the child who is the subject of the report shall not be excluded on the ground that the matter would otherwise be privileged against disclosure under Chapter 49 of NRS. (...49.185 to .275)(1975) includes accountant-client, lawyer-client, school counselor

Table D
ABROGATION OF PRIVILEGED COMMUNICATIONS

States and Territories	All Privileges	Physician Patient	Husband—Wife	Any Similar Privileges	All But Attorney-Client	Social Workers	Psycho-Therapist—Patient Privileges	Ministers	Other[1]
Alabama					X				
Alaska									
Arizona		X	X			X			X
Arkansas		X	X		X				X
California		X			X			X	
Colorado		X							
Connecticut			X						
Delaware		X	X		X	X			X
Dist. of Columbia[2]		X	X						
Florida			X		X		X		
Georgia									
Hawaii		X	X					X	
Idaho		X	X		X			X	X
Illinois	X	X							
Indiana		X	X	X					
Iowa		X							
Kansas		X	X		X				
Kentucky			X		X				
Louisiana		X	X		X			X	
Maine					X				
Maryland		X						X	X
Massachusetts			X						
Michigan			X		X	X	X		
Minnesota									
Mississippi									
Missouri					X				
Montana		X							X
Nebraska		X	X						X
Nevada		X			X			X	
New Hampshire									
New Jersey									X
New Mexico		X	X	X					
New York		X	X	X					
North Carolina		X				X			

40

State													
North Dakota													
Ohio	X												
Oklahoma	X				X							X	
Oregon	X	X	X									X	
Pennsylvania		X											
Rhode Island		X			X							X	
South Carolina	X	X							X				
South Dakota		X							X			X	
Tennessee		X											
Texas	X				X								
Utah													
Vermont													
Virginia	X	X			X								
Washington											X		
West Virginia	X	X			X				X				
Wisconsin		X			X								
Wyoming	X	X			X								
America Samoa	X	X		X	X						X	X	
Guam													
Puerto Rico					X								
Virgin Islands		X											

Numbers refer to footnotes for Tables A through H.

41

and teacher-student, husband-
wife, doctor-patient, confessor-
confessant and news media privilege...

>   -NEV. REV. STAT. §200.506
>   (1979)

Religious Immunity or Exclusion

The religious immunity or spiritual healing
exemption has been the subject of widespread legislative action. In its modern form, the clause
qualifies a statutory definition of neglect or
maltreatment:

>   ...any child who does not re-
>   ceive specific medical treat-
>   ment by reason of the legitimate
>   practice of the religious be-
>   lief of said child's parents,
>   guardian, or others legally
>   responsible for said child,
>   for that reason alone, shall
>   not be considered to be an ab-
>   used or neglected child...

>   -MO. REV. STAT. §210.115(3)
>   (SUPP. 1979)

Despite some commentators' characterization
of these clauses as an impediment to the protection of children, legislative adoption of the
clause has increased from 11 jurisdictions in
1974 to 44 jurisdictions today. They are:

Alabama	Georgia
Alaska	Hawaii
Arizona	Idaho
Arkansas	Illinois
California	Indiana
Colorado	Iowa
Connecticut	Kansas
Delaware	Kentucky
District of Columbia	Louisiana
Florida	Maine

Maryland	Oregon
Massachusetts	Pennsylvania
Michigan	Rhode Island
Minnesota	South Dakota
Mississippi	Utah
Missouri	Vermont
Nevada	Virginia
New Hampshire	Washington
New Jersey	West Virginia
New York	Wisconsin
Ohio	Wyoming
Oklahoma	Guam

Three states, Arizona, Connecticut, and Washington, limit the exception to Christian Science practitioners. Many other states limit the exception to treatment in accordance with the tenets and practices of a recognized or well-recognized church or religious denomination.

In an attempt to balance the conflict between the parents' right to religious freedom and the child's right to live, some states have modified this clause. Alabama, Florida, Kansas, Kentucky, Maine, Michigan, Missouri, and Rhode Island, all explicitly authorize courts to order medical treatment when the child's health requires it. Even without explicit statutory authorization, a court might still have the power to authorize necessary medical treatment.

Penalty for Failure to Report

While it is generally maintained that complete reporting ultimately rests with the concerned response of the community, an additional motive for reporting abuse and neglect is the penalty provision. The following 45 jurisdictions impose a criminal penalty for failure to report:

Alabama	Delaware
Arizona	District of Columbia
Arkansas	Florida
California	Georgia
Colorado	Indiana
Connecticut	Iowa

Kansas	Oregon
Kentucky	Pennsylvania
Louisiana	South Carolina
Maine	South Dakota
Massachusetts	Tennessee
Michigan	Texas
Minnesota	Utah
Missouri	Vermont
Nebraska	Virginia
Nevada	Washington
New Hampshire	West Virginia
New Jersey	Wisconsin
New Mexico	American Samoa
New York	Guam
North Dakota	Puerto Rico
Ohio	Virgin Islands
Oklahoma	

Failure to report is generally a misdemeanor. The typical penalties range from a low of 5 to 30 days in jail and/or a $10 to $100 fine to as high as a year in jail and/or a $1,000 fine. The basis of liability giving rise to a penalty is most often expressed in state law as a "knowing" or "willful" failure to report. The requirement of proving a willful failure to report beyond a reasonable doubt makes the likelihood of a successful prosecution very unlikely. Despite the widespread provision for penalties, there are no reported cases of a criminal prosecution for failure to report an abused or neglected child.

Another incentive for complete reporting is the exposure of mandated reporters to civil liability for damages proximately caused by their failure to report. Five jurisdictions, Arkansas, Colorado, Iowa, New York, and American Samoa, provide for civil liability, in addition to a criminal penalty.

The most celebrated case of civil liability for failure to report is a 1976 California Supreme Court decision, Landeros v. Flood, 17 Cal. 3d 399, 551 P.2d 389. The Court ruled that a doctor who failed to report a child abuse victim can be exposed to liability for subsequent injuries to the child on a theory of medical malpractice. The case involved an 11-month-old girl. She was released by the defendant doctor to her parents after an examination, despite signs of brutality evidenced by unexplained fractures, bruises, and lacerations. The Court held that whether a physician's required standard of care included properly diagnosing and **treating the battered** child syndrome was a question to be decided by a jury on the basis of expert testimony, and not as a matter of law. The issue of whether the intervening injuries were reasonably foreseeable by a prudent physician was held to be a fact to be decided from trial testimony.

Another California case, resulting in a $600,000 settlement, arose when a father brought an action on behalf of his 3-year-old son who had suffered brain damage after repeated beatings by the custodial mother's boyfriend. The child was allegedly examined by four doctors before he was reported as a battered child.

> ...$100 fine and up to 5 days
> in jail and civil liability
> for damages.
>
> > -ARK. STAT. ANN. §42-816
> > (1977)
>
> ...fined not more than five
> hundred dollars or be imprisoned
> for not more than six months,
> or both.
>
> > -S.C. CODE ANN. CH. 10,
> > §20-10-190 (SUPP. 1980)

Reporting Procedures

Table E lists the various procedures that reporters are required to follow. Nearly all jurisdictions require immediate action in reporting. The breakdown of procedures in the jurisdictions is: 25 require oral reports to be followed by written reports; four merely require oral reports;

Table E
REPORTING PROCEDURE

States and Territories	Orally, Followed By Writing	Time When Writing is Due	As Soon As Possible (ASAP) or Not Specified (NS)	Orally Only	Orally or In Writing	Orally, Then In Writing If Requested	Time When Due, If Requested	Procedure Not Specified	Receipt of Report (Social Services Agency)	Law Enforcement Agency	Other Agency
Alabama	X		NS						X	X	X
Alaska			NS					X	X[6]		
Arizona								X	X	X	
Arkansas	X	36 hours				X	48 hours		X		X
California	X								X	X	
Colorado	X								X	X	
Connecticut	X[1]	72 hours							X	X	
Delaware						X	NS[3]		X		
District of Columbia						X	NS		X		
Florida	X		ASAP						X	X	
Georgia						X			X[7]		
Hawaii	X		ASAP			X	NS		X		X
Idaho								X[4]			
Illinois	X	24 hours									
Indiana	X[2]	48 hours		X							
Iowa									X	X	
Kansas						X	NS		X	X	
Kentucky	X	5 days				X	48 hours		X[8]		X
Louisiana						X	48 hours		X	X	
Maine						X			X		
Maryland	X	48 hours							X	X	
Massachusetts	X	48 hours							X		
Michigan	X	72 hours							X		
Minnesota	X		ASAP						X	X	
Mississippi	X		ASAP						X		
Missouri	X	48 hours							X	X	
Montana								X	X		
Nebraska	X		NS						X	X	X

46

State								
Nevada	X					X	X	X
New Hampshire			48 hours	X		X		
New Jersey						X		X
New Mexico	X	48 hours				X[9]		X
New York				X		X		
North Carolina			48 hours	X		X	X	X
North Dakota			NS	X		X		
Ohio						X	X	X
Oklahoma	X	ASAP				X	X	
Oregon		X				X		
Pennsylvania	X	48 hours				X		X
Rhode Island	X	NS				X		X
South Carolina		X				X	X	X
South Dakota		X				X		X
Tennessee	X	5 days			X	X	X	X
Texas	X		48 hours			X	X	X
Utah	X					X	X	
Vermont	X	7 days				X		
Virginia		NS				X		
Washington			NS	X		X	X	
West Virginia			48 hours	X		X		
Wisconsin			NS	X		X	X	X
Wyoming			NS	X		X	X	
America Samoa			48 hours	X				
Guam	X	48 hours			48[5]	X		X
Puerto Rico		48 hours				X		
Virgin Islands			48 hours	X				X

Numbers refer to footnotes for Tables A through H.

two allow the reporter to choose between oral or written reports; 17 require oral reports to be followed by written reports, if requested; and eight require reports, but do not specify the procedure in the reporting law.

Oral reports are to be made "immediately," "promptly," or "as soon as possible." The time within which written reports must follow oral reports ranges from 24 hours to 7 days. The purpose of the oral report is to permit the receiving agency to take immediate protective action if the child's life or health is in danger. The purpose of the written report is to provide a foundation for the investigation and a written record of the report.

States vary somewhat on the required contents of the report. Typically, the reporter is required to state, if known, the names and addresses of the child and his parents or persons having custody of the child and the nature and extent of the child's injuries, including evidence of previous injuries or neglect. A commonly used catch-all phrase reads: "Any other information that the person making the report believes may be helpful in establishing the cause of the injury... . and protecting the child."

Many states require that the reporter make an accusatory report or name the person allegedly responsible for the harm. Others, such as Connecticut and Hawaii, avoid a direct mandate to name the suspected perpetrator by requiring the reporter only to name the "person responsible for the care of the child, if available." Some, such as Arkansas, require both.

To facilitate oral reporting, many local communities and states have established toll-free, 24-hours-a-day reporting hotlines. A number of states established these hotlines through legislation: Arkansas, Maine, Massachusetts, Minnesota, Missouri, New York, Pennsylvania, Virginia, West Virginia, and American Samoa. The hotline simplifies the reporting procedure and provides a trained person to receive the call.

In many jurisdictions statutes designate a
single agency to be responsible for the receipt
and subsequent investigation of reports of child
abuse and neglect. Table E indicates that many
states require that reports be made directly to
the local or state social services department. A
few jurisdictions require reports to be made only
to law enforcement agencies, and many jurisdictions allow reporters to choose between two or more
agencies, typically the social services department or a local law enforcement agency. Thirteen
jurisdictions also allow reports to be made to
other persons or agencies, such as the state's
attorney, district court, probation services
office, or a person or agency designated to be
responsible for the protection of children.

> ...(A) Each report of known
> or suspected child abuse or
> neglect pursuant to this sec-
> tion shall be made immediately
> to the Department's abuse reg-
> istry on the single state-
> wide tollfree telephone num-
> ber or directly to the local
> office of the Department re-
> sponsible for investigation
> of reports made pursuant to
> this section. (B) Each report
> made by a person in an occu-
> pation designated in subsection
> (3) shall be confirmed in
> writing to the local office
> of the Department within 48
> hours of the initial report.
> (C) Reports involving known
> or suspected institutional
> child abuse or neglect shall
> be made and received in the
> same manner as all other re-
> ports made pursuant to this
> section.

-FLA. STAT. §827.07(9)
(1981)

49

> ...shall immediately re-
> port such condition...by
> oral communication and by
> making a written report
> within forty-eight hours
> after such oral communi-
> cation...

> -MASS. GEN. LAW ANN. CH. 119,
> §41A (SUPP. 1981)

> ...The report may be made
> orally, by telephone, or
> in writing...

> -N.C. GEN. STAT. §7A-543
> (SUPP. 1979)

Mandated Action

The majority of state laws require the
agency receiving the report of abuse or neglect
to initiate an investigation "immediately,"
"promptly," or "within 48 hours" and to take
appropriate action to protect the child. Specific
guidelines are usually included in order to assist
in an investigation. The Arkansas law, a typical
example, states:

> The investigation shall include
> the nature, extent and cause of
> the child abuse, sexual abuse
> or neglect; the identity of
> the person responsible therefore;
> the names and conditions of
> other children in the home;
> and evaluation of the parents
> or persons responsible for
> the care of the child; the
> home environment and the re-
> lationship of the child(ren)
> to the parents or other persons
> responsible for their care;
> and all other pertinent data.

> -ARK. STAT. ANN. §42-813(b)
> (1977)

To accomplish these objectives, many states authorize the investigation to include a visit to the child's home, a physical examination of the child, and an interview with the child. If admission to the child's place of residence cannot be obtained, state laws may specifically authorize the court with juvenile jurisdiction, upon good cause shown, to order the person responsible for the child's care to allow the interview, examination, and investigation.

The social services department also is authorized in many states to enlist the assistance of law enforcement agencies or other state agencies in its investigation.

The central element of the investigation is a determination of whether there is probable cause to believe that the child who is the subject of the report is abused or neglected. Expressions of a discernible standard to determine the validity of a report vary from state to state. Some states, such as Oregon, require "reasonable cause to believe." New York requires "some credible evidence of the alleged abuse or maltreatment." Other states, such as South Carolina, require a determination that a report is either "indicated" or "unfounded"; an indicated report is one "supported by facts which warrant a finding that abuse or neglect is more likely than not to have occurred."

If the investigation indicates that child abuse or neglect has occurred, the social services department must determine what services and further action would be appropriate. The Wyoming law, for example, states:

> The local child protection
> agency shall...(iv) if the
> investigation discloses that
> child abuse or neglect is
> present, initiate services
> with the family of the abused

> or neglected child to assist
> in resolving problems that
> lead to or caused the child
> abuse or neglect.

> —WYO. STAT. §14-3-204(a)

If the investigation indicates that there is reasonable cause to believe that the child is in immediate danger, many states, such as Massachusetts and Connecticut, authorize the immediate removal of the child from his surroundings.

The investigating department may also be given discretion or mandated to forward a copy of its findings to an appropriate agency for possible legal action. The Wyoming law, for example, states:

> The local child protection
> agency shall: ...(vi) when
> the best interest of the
> child require court action,
> contact the county and pro-
> secuting attorney to initiate
> proceedings.

> —WYO. STAT. §14-3240(a)

To assist the social services department with identification, investigation, and disposition of reported cases of child abuse and neglect, several states have legislatively established child protection teams. The teams are comprised of members with a variety of expertise, such as social services workers, physicians, nurses, attorneys, mental health professionals, and lay representatives of the community. The responsibilities of the team may vary from state to state. In several states, such as Massachusetts, Michigan, Missouri, Pennsylvania, South Carolina, and Utah, the social services department has the option of utilizing the team's expertise. The department may ask the team to assist in investigations and in the planning and providing of protective services. In other states, such as Tennessee, the team is required to review each report of suspected child abuse and make recommendations to the department of social services, and is permitted to file a petition in the juvenile court on behalf of an abused child.

Investigation of Institutional Abuse and Neglect

Institutional abuse and neglect generally refers to situations in which the person responsible for a child's welfare is not the biological parent. These include foster homes, private institutions, or governmental residential facilities. The incidence of child maltreatment in such settings is significant. Many states attempt to insure that investigations will be independent and thorough when the agency responsible for the investigation is related administratively to the institution in which the alleged harm took place. A number of states incorporate clauses into their legislation to insure such independence in investigations: Alabama, District of Columbia, Florida, Georgia, Indiana, Kansas, Michigan, Minnesota, Nevada, Oklahoma, Pennsylvania, South Carolina, Utah, Vermont, Virginia, Wisconsin, Guam, Puerto Rico, and the Virgin Islands.

Other states have adopted administrative procedures to implement this standard. Examples of the language used in the law are:

> If there is reasonable cause to suspect that a child in the care of or under the control of a public or private agency, institution, or facility is an abused or neglected child, the agency, institution, or facility shall be investigated by an agency administratively independent of the agency, institution, or facility being investigated.

-MICH. COMP. LAWS ANN. §722.628(4) (SUPP. 1981)

If an employee of the local
department is suspected of
abusing or neglecting a child,
the report shall be made to
the juvenile and domestic
relations court of the county
or city where the abuse or
neglect was discovered.

-VA. CODE §63.1-248.3(A)
(1981)

Central Registry

A central registry is a single depository of
information about suspected and known cases of
child abuse and/or neglect in a given jurisdiction.
One aspect of reporting laws in 44 jurisdictions
developed in the last decade has been the mandating of central registries. Table F illustrates
those 44 jurisdictions that have legislatively
provided for a central registry system. In addition, several jurisdictions maintain a centralized
record of child abuse reports as a matter of administrative policy: Georgia, Indiana, Kansas,
Kentucky, Minnesota, North Dakota, and West Virginia. Central registries receive and store data
about maltreated children and about persons responsible for their condition.

Except in California, where the registry is
within the Department of Justice, all state laws
place central registries within the structure of
the state department of welfare or social services.
Most jurisdictions provide for one registry located at the state level. A few states, such as New
York and Tennessee, require both state and county
registries.

Statutory provisions that establish central
registers are important (1) because of the degree
to which such statutory references structure and
define administrative procedures for operating
registries; (2) because many states have moved

to specific legislation to authorize their registries, as opposed to merely establishing them
through administrative decisions; and (3) because
it is in the statutory provisions that the basic
civil liberties protections are found.

The District of Columbia law exemplifies the
kind of purposes and uses which may be made of
the central registry:

> The purposes of the Register
> are to:
>
> (1) maintain a confidential
> index of cases of abused and
> neglected children;
> (2) assist in the identifi-
> cation and treatment of abused
> children and their families;
> and
> (3) serve as a resource for
> the evaluation, management,
> planning of programs and ser-
> vices ...
>
> > -D.C. CODE ANN. §2111(b)
> > (SUPP. 1978)

The Iowa law states:

> The purposes...are to facil-
> itate the identification of
> victims or potential victims
> of child abuse by making a-
> vailable a single, statewide
> source of child abuse data;
> to facilitate research on
> child abuse...; and to pro-
> vide maximum safeguards a-
> gainst unwarranted invasions
> of privacy which such a reg-
> istry might otherwise entail.
>
> > -IOWA CODE ANN. §235A.12

In the 44 jurisdictions which have legislated

Table F
CENTRAL REGISTRIES MANDATED BY STATUTES

Category	Alabama	Alaska	Arizona	Arkansas	California	Colorado	Connecticut	Delaware	Dist of Columbia	Florida	Georgia	Hawaii	Idaho	Illinois	Indiana	Iowa	Kansas	Kentucky	Louisiana	Maine	Maryland	Massachusetts
Other Information Authorized to be Included	X			X					X													
Follow-up Reports Included	X			X					X								X					
Reports Describing Results of All Investigations & Initial Reports Included	X		X	X													X					
Reports Describing the Results of "Founded" or "Indicated" Investigations Included									X[5]													
Reports Describing Results of All Investigations Included			X						X													
Only Initial Reporter's Report Included				X[4]	X										X							
Statute Silent About Types of Reports in Registry					X							X	X						X		X[6]	
Central Registry Mandated by Statute	X	X	X	X	X	X	X	X[7]	X	X		X	X	X		X			X		X	X[1]

State								
Michigan	X	X						
Minnesota	X							X
Mississippi	X[2]							
Missouri	X	X			X		X	
Montana	X	X						
Nebraska	X		X					
Nevada	X	X		X			X	
New Hampshire	X	X						
New Jersey	X	X						
New Mexico								
New York	X	X						
North Carolina	X	X			X		X	X
North Dakota								
Ohio	X	X		X				
Oklahoma	X			X				
Oregon	X				X			
Pennsylvania	X	X			X			
Rhode Island	X	X			X			
South Carolina	X				X			
South Dakota	X[3]							
Tennessee	X[2]	X						
Texas	X							
Utah	X							
Vermont	X				X	X	X	X
Virginia	X	X			X		X	X
Washington	X	X						
West Virginia	X							
Wisconsin	X			X				
Wyoming	X[8]				X	X		X
American Samoa	X				X		X	X
Guam	X				X	X	X	X
Puerto Rico							X	X
Virgin Islands							X	X

Numbers refer to footnotes for Tables A through H.

their central registries, 38 provide for one
register located at the state level although
Maryland also specifically permits local county
registries. Tennessee and New York require both
state and county registries. Nevada mandates a
register within the central office of the welfare
division and allows the division to designate
county-run hospitals in counties of over 100,000
people to act as regional registries. Delaware
requires a register in each county.

In 17 of the jurisdictions the laws delineate
what categories of information should or can be
placed in the registry. A typical statute declares:

> The central registry shall
> contain but shall not be limit-
> ed to: (a) All information
> in any written report received
> under this article; (b) Re-
> cord of the final disposition
> of the report, including serv-
> ices offered and services
> accepted; (c) The plan for
> rehabilitative treatment; (d)
> The name and identifying data,
> date, and circumstances of any
> person requesting or receiving
> information from the central
> registry; (e) Any other in-
> formation which might be help-
> ful in furthering the purpose
> of this article.
>
> —COLO. REV. STAT. §19-10-
> 114(1)(2) (1978)

Fifteen statutes do not describe the categories of data to be placed in the registry. Four
states include only the initial reporters' reports.
Two states include only the reports of all "indicated" or "founded" investigations, while three
states include these reports and follow-up reports.
Three states include all investigatory reports, and
one other includes all investigatory reports plus
follow-up reports. One state retains all initial

reports and investigation reports; seven other jurisdictions include all initial reports, investigation reports, and follow-up reports. Seven authorize the inclusion of "other" information.

Only two jurisdictions, the District of Columbia and Pennsylvania, have legislatively mandated two separate files to handle different categories of reports. In the District of Columbia, information on unsupported reports is kept in a separate index with the identifying characteristics destroyed. In Pennsylvania, there is a pending complaint file of reports under investigation and a central registry consisting of founded and indicated reports. When an investigation determines that a report is founded or indicated, all information is expunged from the pending file and an entry is made in the central register (expunction is discussed below). If a report is unfounded, all information is expunged from the pending file. The statute also gives the department the power to keep some data on unfounded reports for statistical purposes.

Destruction, Sealing, Expunction, and Amendment of Central Registry Data

Over a period of time, the situation within a family changes. The central registry's records must reflect these changes or the use of out-of-date information will constitute an infringement of the rights of those persons whose names and actions are recorded in the data bank.

Destruction of a record ensures that there is no possibility of revival of the complete file of a particular case. Sealing means that a record is removed from the registry and placed in a sealed envelope or container and placed in a secure, segregated place, with access prohibited. Expunction is the physical erasure or obliteration of information. There is no possibility of future retrieval; the document or file might survive, however. Amending a record is the adding or subtracting of information in light of a new information or corrections brought to the attention of the

Table G
DESTRUCTION, EXPUNCTION, SEALING, AMENDMENT OF STATUTORY CENTRAL REGISTER INFORMATION

Action	Alabama	Alaska	Arizona	Arkansas	California	Colorado	Connecticut	Delaware	Dist of Columbia	Florida	George	Hawaii	Idaho	Illinois	Indiana	Iowa	Kansas	Kentucky	Louisiana	Maine	Maryland	Massachusetts	Michigan	Minnesota
HEAD OF DEPARTMENT MAY AMEND, SEAL OR EXPUNGE RECORDS				X[13]		X[13]																		
PERSON LISTED IN REGISTER HAS RIGHT TO HEARING ON REQUEST TO AMEND, SEAL OR EXPUNGE				X		X											X				X		X	
PERSON LISTED IN REGISTER MAY REQUEST AMENDMENT, SEALING OR EXPUNCTION				X		X			X[12]								X				X		X	
PERSON LISTED GIVEN NOTICE TO THEIR RIGHTS TO CHALLENGE CONTENTS OF FILES									X															
PERSONS LISTED GIVEN NOTICE THAT THEY ARE IN THE REGISTER									X												X			
ACTION TAKEN IF A REPORT IS UNFOUNDED				X[4]		X[4]			X[4]	X[4]							X[1]						X[7]	X[4]
ACTION TAKEN WHEN 10 YEARS HAVE ELAPSED SINCE LAST REPORT																X[3]								
ACTION TAKEN WHEN 7 YEARS ELAPSED SINCE LAST REPORT									X[6]								X[6]							
ACTION TAKEN NO LATER THAN WHEN A CHILD REACHES 21				X[3]		X[3]																		
ACTION TAKEN WHEN A CHILD REACHES AGE 18		X[1]		X[2]		X[2]			X[5]														X	X[3]

60

State													
Mississippi													
Missouri													
Montana													
Nebraska		X^3											
Nevada				X^4 X^1									
New Hampshire													
New Jersey													
New Mexico	X^2	X^3		X^4	X	X	X						
New York											X		X^{13}
North Carolina													
North Dakota													
Ohio													
Oklahoma													
Oregon	X^4			X^4	X	X	X				X		X^{13}
Pennsylvania													
Rhode Island			X^4		X	X	X						
South Carolina													
South Dakota													
Tennessee	X^{10}												
Texas													
Utah	X^{11}												
Vermont				X^1		X			X		X		
Virginia													
Washington													
West Virginia													
Wisconsin				X^1									
Wyoming	X^2	X^3		X^4									
American Samoa													
Guam						X	X.		X		X		X^{13}
Puerto Rico													
Virgin Islands													

Numbers refer to footnotes for Tables A through H.

Table H

CENTRAL REGISTER INFORMATION RELEASE PROCEDURES

CENTRAL REGISTER INFORMATION MAY BE RELEASED:

	Alabama	Alaska	Arizona	Arkansas	California	Colorado	Connecticut	Delaware	Florida	Georgia	Hawaii	Idaho	Illinois	Indiana	Iowa	Kansas	Kentucky	Louisiana	Maine	Maryland
ALL DISCLOSURES NEED APPROVAL			X										X							
TO A STATE OR COUNTY ATTORNEY					X				X											
TO OTHER PERSONS AS A COURT ORDER						X														
PERSONS ENGAGED IN BONA FIDE RESEARCH WITH NO IDENTIFYING INFORMATION OF SUBJECTS GIVEN UNLESS STATE APPROVED	X				X				X[5]X						X					
TO ANY STATE OR LOCAL OFFICIAL RESPONSIBLE FOR CHILD PROTECTION OR LEGISLATION		X			X				X						X			X		X
TO A GRAND JURY	X																			
TO A COURT FOR IN-CAMERA INSPECTION UNLESS IT DETERMINES PUBLIC DISCLOSURE IS NECESSARY	X[2]	X	X[2]	X	X[2]	X	X								X[2,7]					
TO ANY PERSON RESPONSIBLE FOR A CHILD, WITH PROTECTION FOR THE IDENTIFICATION OF PERSONS					X			X												
TO ANY PERSON NAMED IN REPORT; IF HE IS A MINOR OR INCOMPETENT, TO HIS GUARDIAN AD LITEM	X[1]			X			X								X[6]					
TO AN AGENCY AUTHORIZED TO TREAT/SUPERVISE A CHID OR PARENT/GUARDIAN			X	X	X					X					X[6]					X
TO A PERSON WITH AUTHORITY TO TAKE A CHILD INTO PROTECTIVE CUSTODY				X											X					
TO A PHYSICIAN WHO HAS A CHILD BEFORE HIM	X		X	X		X			X						X					X
TO POLICE OR LAW ENFORCEMENT AGENCY INVESTIGATING A REPORT	X		X		X	X		X												
TO A CHILD PROTECTIVE AGENCY INVESTIGATING A REPORT TREATING A CHILD/FAMILY		X	X		X	X		X	X	X					X					X
LAW PROVIDES SPECIFIC EXCEPTIONS TO CONFIDENTIALITY	X	X	X[3]	X	X	X	•	•	X	X	X	•	•	X		X		X		X[3]

State														
Massachusetts	X	X		X	X	X	X	X			X			X
Michigan	X			X	X									
Minnesota	X	X		X	X						X			
Mississippi	X		X	X	X	X		X^2		X			X	X
Missouri	X	X										X	X	
Montana	X^4	X		X	X	X		X^3		X				
Nebraska	X^4			X	X	X	X							
Nevada												X		
New Hampshire	X^4	X		X	X	X	X		X^8	X				
New Jersey	X			X	X	X				X				
New Mexico	X		X	X	X	X^7		X^3	X^1	X				
New York	X			X	X									
North Carolina	4													
North Dakota														
Ohio	X	X		X	X						X			
Oklahoma	X	X	X											
Oregon	X	X^9	X			X^6		X^3	X	X		X		
Pennsylvania	X	X^9						X^3						
Rhode Island	X													
South Carolina	X	X	X											
South Dakota	X													
Tennessee	4													
Texas	4													
Utah	X					X^6				X		X		
Vermont	X	X^{10}												
Virginia	4				X	X				X				
Washington	X	X	X											
West Virginia														
Wisconsin	X						X			X				
Wyoming	X^4	X	X	X	X	X^5		X^2	X^5	X		X^2		X
American Samoa	X^4	X	X	X	X	X^6		X^2	X^5	X		X^2		X
Guam	X	X^{11}												
Puerto Rico														
Virgin Islands														

63

Numbers refer to footnotes for Tables A through H. (see Footnotes for Table G).

agency responsible for maintaining the central registry.

Table H shows that only 18 jurisdictions which have set up their central registers by statute have provided in their reporting laws for the destruction, sealing, expunction, and amendment of information in these data systems. For the most part, these jurisdictions have the most extensive reporting laws and the most detailed sections mandating the operations of the central registry. Others may have provided this function in departmental regulations or in statutory sections detailing the handling of all records held by state agencies.

In many states, all initial reports of suspected abuse and neglect are contained in the central register for only a limited period of time. By or before the expiration of this time period, pursuant to an investigation by the local agency, the report would have to be converted into a "founded" or "unfounded" (or possibly an "indicated") category. Many reports that are received and stored, and made accessible prove to be unfounded; they might be made by malicious relatives or neighbors or, more commonly, by well-intentioned reporters who are mistaken. If no findings are made within the time period, the report will automatically be converted into an unfounded report.

This time limitation forces protective services to make a prompt formal decision. Verifying reports of suspected cases of abuse and neglect is usually a difficult task. Most state laws do not give the workers any assistance in their determination of whether they have enough evidence to label a case as founded. Most laws do not provide a standard for the quantum of proof necessary. In statutes that do provide a standard of proof, the tests range from "probable cause," _i.e._, Tennessee, to "some credible evidence," _i.e._, Arkansas. The lowest quantum of proof is a "mere scintilla of evidence" which means any piece of evidence at all that would lead a person to suspect that child abuse or neglect had taken place. At the other end of the spectrum is "beyond a

reasonable doubt" which means that the facts
prove the presence of abuse or neglect to a certainty. In between, ranging from the least to
most stringent are: "some credible evidence,"
"reasonable cause to suspect," "reasonable cause
to believe," probable cause to believe," mere
preponderance of the evidence," "fair preponderance of the evidence," and "clear and convincing evidence."

The retention of unfounded reports might
cause innocent adults to suffer at some later
date. Future users of a central registry may not
always be told that a report was unfounded. Just
the listing of a name carries with it a stigma of
guilt which could be damaging. Four states destroy
all records if there is an unfounded report. But
more states feel that the report itself should remain for purposes of data gathering and policy review; therefore, ten jurisdictions expunge the
names of other identifying characteristics in unfounded reports (see Column 5 of Table G).

It has been argued that since the purpose of
the central registry is to help protect the health
and welfare of children, there would be no need
to maintain records after the child reaches the
age of majority and is able to protect himself/
herself. Therefore, all records should be destroyed
at that time. However, only two states mandate
this action. Other states have adopted different
variations because they are concerned that abuse
and neglect is a family heritage that is passed
on from generation to generation. Records that
are maintained beyond the time that the child
reaches the age of 18 may be of use in the future
for prevention and treatment. Four states seal all
records no later than when the subject reaches the
age of 28. Four specifically provide that the
files can be opened only if a sibling or offspring
is reported to be abused or neglected. Six states,
instead of sealing or destroying records after a
specific time period has passed, provide for the
expunction of identifying information if certain
conditions have been satisfied (see columns 1
through 4 of Table H).

In only five states do the reporting laws
require that persons listed in the central registries be told that they are in the data system;
four of these also require that the subjects be
told of their right to challenge the content of
their files. In six other jurisdictions, even
though protective service workers are not required
to inform subjects of reports that their names
have been placed into the central registry, the
subjects have the right to request amendment,
sealing, or expunction of their records. Nine
jurisdictions give subjects of reports the right
to a hearing if their request to change a record
is denied (see Columns 6 through 9 of Table G).

Reporting Child Sexual Abuse

Today, 48 states, the District of Columbia,
and all U.S. territories specifically include
"sexual abuse" in their reporting law definitions.
As of this publication, the two which have not
included sexual abuse in their reporting statute
definitions of child abuse or neglect are South
Dakota and Tennessee.

Ten states, American Samoa, and Guam define
sexual abuse in their reporting laws by referral
to their criminal sexual offense statutes. These
states are: California, Indiana, Michigan, Minnesota, North Carolina, Oklahoma, South Carolina,
and Wyoming. At least two states, Maryland and
Nevada, define what acts constitute sexual abuse
in the reporting law definitional provisions.
Maryland's definition of sexual abuse is "any
act or acts involving sexual molestation or exploitation, including but not limited to incest,
rape, or sexual offense in any degree, sodomy
or unnatural or perverted sexual practices on a
child." Md. Code Ann. art. 27, Section 35A(b)(8)
(Supp. 1978). Nevada's definition states: "Sexual
abuse includes but is not limited to acts upon a
child constituting the crimes of: (a) Incest...
(b) The infamous crime against nature... (c)
Lewdness with a child... (d) Annoyance or molestation of a minor... (e) Sadomasochistic abuse...
(f) Sexual assault... (g) Statutory sexual seduc-

tion." 1979 Nev. Stats. ch.290. New York's reporting law definition of sexual abuse refers to the definition found in its Family Court Act.

The trend is to make sexual abuse by a parent or caretaker a form of child abuse which must be reported if suspected. However, some states' reporting law definitions of sexual abuse do not limit the reportable abuse to that which is caused by a parent or person responsible for the child's care. Among such states are: Alabama, Alaska, Arkansas, California, Colorado, Delaware, Hawaii, Louisiana, Nebraska, New Hampshire, New York, Ohio, Oregon, and Wisconsin. In fact, some states require reporting only a parent's or caretaker's neglect, but require reports of abuse caused by any person. Wisconsin is an example of this requirement. Wis. Stat. Ann. Section 48.981(a),(d) (West. Supp. 1980).

But there may be justification for requiring reporting of abuse by any person. Child abuse, including sexual abuse, may still be perpetrated by someone related to or close to the family, although such person is not responsible for the child's care. A classic example is the mother's boyfriend who visits or stays in the home on a regular basis, or a teenage neighbor who is the child of family friends.

On the other hand, in states which limit reporting of abuse (or neglect) by a caretaker, there is a strong likelihood that instances of abuse by persons close to the family still would be reported. This is because the caretaker's "neglect" in failing to exercise proper care and protection to prevent or stop the abuse would be reportable. As a result, the child would be adequately protected through reporting of the caretaker's conduct. Further, the requirement of reporting abuse by any person technically would cover situations involving complete strangers. This appears to go beyond the purpose of child abuse and neglect laws, which seek to protect children from harm within their family. As a practical matter, however, such situations, at

67

least where sexual abuse is involved, statisti-
cally do not represent the typical case. Available
data suggests that at least 75% of sexual abuse
of children is perpetrated by persons known to
the child, including relatives or close acquaintances. Moreover, where a complete stranger is
the perpetrator, the caretaker(s) probably would
report the abuse to the authorities and make other
efforts to protect or provide treatment for the
child.

FOOTNOTES FOR TABLES A THROUGH H

TABLE A- Who Reports

1. Jurisdictions requiring reports of child abuse from "practitioners of the Healing Arts" imply that all medical professionals must report. If a statute enumerates specific medical professions, in addition to "practitioners," these were checked in the appropriate column as well. Similarly, some states require reports of abuse from "any person, such as . . . or including, but not limit- ed to . . . ." In such cases, each party listed was checked as well as the "Any other Person" column.

2. The following have been designated under both the "Teacher" and "Other School Personnel" columns because of the statutes' inference: Arizona, Colo- rado, Delaware, Iowa, Nebraska, and Oregon refer to school personnel or employees; Minnesota refers to "a professional or his delegate who is engaged in the practice of . . . education."

3. All jurisdictions checked in the "Religious Healing Practitioner" column, except for Alaska, California, and Ohio, refer to Christian Scien- tists, South Carolina and West Virginia refer to both Christian Scientists and religious healing practitioners.

4. Other specifically named persons not listed by a separate heading in Table A, but required to report include: Alabama - sanitarium; Alaska - health aide, physical therapist, and Officers of the Division of Corrections; Colorado - child health associates; Illinois - truant officer, social services administrator, and Illinois De- partment of Public Aid; Kentucky - health profes- sional; Maryland - professional employee of a

correctional institution and state trooper; Massachusetts - guidance or family counselor; Michigan - audiologist; Missouri - juvenile officer; New Hampshire - therapist; North Carolina - public health worker; Ohio - speech pathologist or audiologist; Oregon - employee of the Department of Human Resources, county health department, community mental health program, and county·juvenile department; Vermont - physicians' assistants; Washington - employee of the Department of social and health services.

TABLE B- Immunity

1. Michigan's immunity section extends to "assisting in any other requirement of this act," and Section 722,626 (1), (2) (Supp. 1978) authorizes physicians to detain endangered children in protective custody and to take X-rays and photographs.

2. West Virginia's immunity extends to "any act permitted or required by this article," and Section 49-6A-4 authorizes any person required to report to take photographs and X-rays at public expense.

3. Wyoming's immunity extends to "any act required or permitted" and Section 14-3-206(c) allows any person investigating, examining, or treating suspected child abuse or neglect to take photographs and X-rays.

4. The Virgin Islands' immunity extends to "any act permitted or required by this chapter," and Section 175 authorizes mandatory reporters to take photographs and X-rays; Section 176(a) authorizes police and physicians to take protective custody of children.

TABLE D - Abrogation of Privileged Communications

1. The thirteen jurisdictions included in the "Other" column are: Arizona and Delaware - "any privilege . . . provided for by professions such as nursing covered by law or a code of ethics regarding practioner-client confidences . . .; Ark-

ansas, Idaho, Pennsylvania, and American Samoa -
"any privilege . . . between any professional person. . . including . . . counselors, hospitals,
clinics, day care centers, and schools and their
clients;" Louisiana and South Catolina- "any privilege . . . between any professional person and
his client . . .;" Maryland- "every health prac-
tioner, educator or . . . law enforcement officer,
who contacts, examines, attends, or treats a child
and who believes. . . the child has been abused
is required to make a report . . . notwithstanding
any other section . . . relating to privileged
communications . . .;" Massachusetts - "any privilege established . . . by court decision or by
profession code relating to the exclusion of confidential communications and the competency of witnesses . . .;" Nevada - "shall not be excluded on
the grounds that the matter would be privileged .
, . under chapter 49 of Nevada Revised Statutes
(which includes accountant-client, lawyer-client,
school counselor and teacher-student) . . . and
the news media privilege . . .;" Oregon - "the
privilege extended to staff members of schools
and to nurses . . .;" and South Dakota - "school
counselor and student."

TABLE E - Reporting Procedure

1. Connecticut - In addition to Section 17-38a(c),
which is reflected in Table E, Connecticut law
has several variations in its reporting procedure:
Section 17-38b states that "Any of the persons .
. . described in subsection (b) of section 17-38a
having reasonable cause to believe that any child
. . . is in danger of being abused, but who does
not have reasonable cause to suspect any such
abuse has actually occurred, shall immediately
cause a written report to be made . . ." And
Section 17-38c states that "Any person other than
those enumerated in subsection (b) of section 17-
38a having reasonable cause to suspect or believe
that any child . . . is in danger of being abused
or neglected . . . or has been so abused or neglected shall immediately cause a written or oral
report to be made . . ."

71

2. Iowa - ". . .Each report made by a mandatory
reporter . . . shall be made both orally and in
writing. Each report made by a permissive reporter
. . . may be oral, written, or both . . ."

3. Delaware - ". . . in accordance with rules and
regulations of the Division of Social Services .
. ."

4. Idaho - ". . . within twenty-four hours. . ."

5. Puerto Rico - ". . .by the quickest means of
communication, within a period of not more than
48 hours after the minor's condition is known."

6. Alaska - "If the person making a report . . .
cannot reasonably contact the nearest office of
the department, and immediate action is necessary
for the well-being of the child, the person shall
make the report to a peace officer . . ."

7. Georgia - ". . . to a child welfare agency providing protective services . . . or, in the absence
of such agency, to an appropriate police authority
. . ."

8. Kentucky - ". . . to the Bureau. . . If the
person making the report has reason to believe
that immediate protection for the child is advisable, the person shall also make an oral report
to an appropriate law enforcement agency."

9. New York - ". . . Oral reports . . . to the
statewide central register . . . unless the . . .
local plan . . . provides that oral reports should
be made to the local child protective service. . .
Written reports shall be made to the appropriate
child protective service. . ."

TABLE F - Central Registries Mandated by Statutes

1. The central registry contains "data sufficient
to identify children whose names are reported. . ."

2. The central registry contains only the name,

address, and age of each child; the nature of the harm reported; and the name and address of the person responsible for the care of the child.

3. The central registry contains the reports of court actions only.

4. The central registry contains reports of physical injury only as well as arrests for, and convictions of violations of Section 273a.

5. The central registry contains the initial reports of "founded" or "indicated" investigations also.

6. The name of any person may not be entered unless he has been adjudicated a child abuser, has unsuccessfully appealed the entry through Department procedures, or has failed to respond to notification that his name would be entered.

7. "Information concerning each case of abuse or neglect" is included.

8. The central registry contains reports "under investigation," "founded," or "closed."

TABLE G - Destruction, Expunction, Sealing, Amendment of Statutory Central Register Information

1. All records are destroyed.

2. There will be access to the records only if a sibling or offspring is reported to have been abused or neglected.

3. All records are sealed.

4. Identifying information will be expunged.

5. Identifying information will be expunged when the child is 18 years old, if there is no reasonable suspicion or evidence that a younger sibling is abused or neglected, or at the end of the fifth year after the termination of services directed toward the abuse or neglect, whichever occurs

first.

6. Identifying information will be expunged seven years after the last report unless the individual continues to be a client of the Department, in which case there is no expunction.

7. If requested by a suspected abuser, that person's name will be expunged if no entry has been made for seven previous years.

8. Identifying information will be expunged when the child reaches 18 years of age, or one year after the termination of services, whichever occurs first.

9. Identifying information will be expunged when the child reaches 18 years of age or ten years after the last report, whichever occurs later.

10. The department is given the power to adopt rules providing for the "purging of reports upon a child's reaching 18 years of age."

11. Records relating to an individual child are destroyed when the child reaches the age of 18. Records relating to the family or sibling are destroyed when the youngest sibling reaches the age of 18.

12. "The Mayor shall establish, by rules . . . ., procedures to permit a person . . . to challenge information which he or she alleges is incorrect."

13. The information may be amended, expunged, or sealed "upon good cause shown" and with notice to the subject of the report."

   Note: Numbers in table.H apply to
         notes appearing here in Ex-
         planatory Notes G supra.

Chapter 3
JUDICIAL ASPECTS OF CHILD ABUSE AND NEGLECT

Agencies Mandated to Receive Reports of Abuse and Neglect

A review of reporting laws indicate that in 22 states and 2 territories the department of social services was the sole agency mandated to receive reports of child abuse and neglect. In 26 states and the District of Columbia the department of social services and other agencies, usually law enforcement, are mandated to receive reports.

Agencies Responsible for Investigating Reports

In 34 states and 2 territories the agency responsible for investigating reports is the public social services agency or its representative. In 15 states and the District of Columbia the public social services agency shares the investigative responsibility with other agencies, such as law enforcement, the juvenile court and the probation department. In the remaining state, Georgia, the reporting law does not specify the agency responsible for investigation reports.

Protective Custody

The previous chapter briefly mentioned the provisions found in state reporting laws that allow the emergency removal and temporary custody of children without parental consent or decree of the court in order to protect the child from further abuse or injury.

Most jurisdictions authorize police to remove from the home a child in imminent danger of extreme abuse. A growing number of states now extend this protective custody power to child protection agencies, for example: Alabama, Alaska,

Arizona, Arkansas, Connecticut, Florida, Maryland, Massachusetts, Montana, New Jersey, New York, Texas, Virginia, and American Samoa.

An even greater number of jurisdictions extend protective custody powers to hospitals when a physician believes it is necessary to retain the child in order to protect him from further injury: Alabama, Arkansas, Connecticut, Florida, Illinois, Kentucky, Michigan, Missouri, New Jersey, New York, North Carolina, North Dakota, Pennsylvania, Rhode Island, Tennessee, Utah, Virginia, Washington, Wyoming, American Samoa, and the Virgin Islands.

The authorization in these situations usually limits the custodial period from 24 to 72 hours or until the next session of a family or juvenile court.

Most states limit the circumstances in which a child can be placed in protective custody. States that allow removal without a court order require that authorized persons have reasonable cause to believe that the child is in imminent danger, and that there is not time to secure a court order. Similar limitations are imposed by the Fourth Amendment to the Constitution, which prohibits unreasonable seizures. In states that require a court order prior to removal, the person requesting the order must establish that immediate harm may occur to a child unless the order is issued.

Most states require that the parents of children taken into custody be notified immediately and that a petition be filed for a formal hearing within some fixed period of time. These requirements attempt to balance the rights of the parents and the welfare of the child. The issue of parental rights versus the welfare of the child remains a controversial and unsettled one in child protection law.

Another restriction, which attaches to the protective custody process in a growing number of states, prohibits placing abused or neglected

children in any adult detention facility. Several
states also forbid placing abused or neglected
children in any detention facility.

Deciding Whether to Go to Court*

One of the most difficult questions child
protection service workers or attorneys face is
deciding when to go to court. Serious abuse and/
or neglect clearly warrants the use of the court's
authority for the child's protection. But in many
cases, particularly those involving neglect as
distinguished from abuse, the decision regarding
whether to go to court is less clear-cut or com-
pelling.

Court action is usually considered to remove
a child temporarily or permanently from the home
or to obtain adequate treatment when (1) the child
is in imminent danger and/or (2) attempts at treatment have been unsuccessful, and the parents have
made no progress toward providing adequate care
for the child. In this situation the child remains
in a very unhealthy home environment, even though
every possible avenue for ameliorating the situation has been explored.

Court intervention may be required in cases
where:

      (1) families refuse to cooperate
          with the investigation and
          there is reason to suspect
          that a situation of abuse
          and neglect exists;

      (2) families are unwilling to
          accept needed services al-

---

*Source: Child Protection: The Role of the
Courts, developed by H.R. Landau, M.K. Salus,
and T. Stiffarm with N.L. Kalb, edited by
Kirschner Associates, Inc., for the National
Center on Child Abuse and Neglect, U.S. Department of Health and Human Services, Washington (1980)

> though their child is in
> substantial danger;

(3) the investigation indicates
the need for removal of the
child;

(4) the family is eligible for
services only if the child
is a dependent of the court.

Court intervention may also be required if the
family is already under authority of the court
and a modification of the court order is necessary to terminate the parental rights of the natural parents.

The Court System

There are two types of courts: criminal and
civil. Either or both courts may be involved in
a child abuse and neglect case. Juvenile courts
are civil courts and thus may not have the rigidity
of practice and procedure which ordinarily exists
in a criminal court. Child abuse and neglect is
usually dealt with in the juvenile court process
where the focus is upon the welfare of the child
in the total context of the family. The name of
the court varies from state to state. It may be
called "children's court," the "family court," or
the "domestic relations court." The title "juvenile
court" will be used as a generic term throughout
this discussion.

In some states, the juvenile court is a separate court or division distinct from the total
court system, although there is a trend toward a
unified court system.

Courts have two major interests when dealing
with child abuse and neglect cases. The first of
these is _protection_ of the child. This is usually
accomplished through _civil procedures_ in a juvenile

court. The second is <u>criminal prosecution</u> of the abusive or neglectful parent or custodian or guardian.

Criminal Court*

Criminal prosecution of abusive or neglectful parents may be instituted under criminal statutes that deal with such actions as <u>assault</u>, <u>battery</u>, <u>contributing to the delinquency of a minor</u>, <u>sexual abuse</u>, or <u>homicide</u>. Some states have created a separate crime of child abuse or cruelty to children. Regardless of the specific statute, in a <u>criminal prosecution</u> for child abuse or neglect, the defendant is entitled to the full protections guaranteed by the Fourth, Fifth and Sixth Amendments of the Constitution, including right to jury, strict adherence to the rules of evidence, right to cross-examination, right to appointed counsel, right to a public and speedy trial, and the highest standard of proof (that is, beyond a reasonable doubt). Similarly, the criminal <u>investigation</u> of child abuse or neglect is subject to the strict constraints imposed by the Constitution. These are put into effect by the exclusionary rule which provides that evidence obtained in violation of constitutional provisions may not be used for criminal prosecution.

Criminal prosecution may result in such penalties as probation or incarceration in a penal institution, but criminal courts have no authority to make orders concerning the child victim. Thus, criminal jurisdiction is directed at deterring or rehabilitating the defendant abuser or neglector rather than at ensuring the safety of the child.

Juvenile Court

The authority and jurisdiction of the juvenile court emanate from state law. In most states,

---

* Adapted from material developed by B.A. Caulfield in <u>The Legal Aspects of Protective Services for Abused and Neglected Children</u>, U.S. Department of Health and Human Services, Washington, D.C. (1978).

the juvenile court has exclusive responsibility or jurisdiction over many family- and child-related legal problems. The juvenile court has jurisdiction over minors in delinquency cases, status offenders (children in need of supervision and runaways), and children who are maltreated, dependent, or neglected. The maximum age at which an individual is still considered a minor varies from 16 to 18 years depending on the state, and the court may have continuing jurisdiction until age 21.

The juvenile court, when hearing cases of child abuse and/or neglect, is a <u>civil</u> court. As such, the essential responsibility or purpose of the court is to protect the minor(s) from further risk of abuse or neglect. Juvenile courts have a range of dispositions available to them which are intended to protect the child and to rehabilitate the child and the family. The most extreme is permanent removal of the child from the home and termination of parental rights. Others include temporary removal while the parents undergo therapy, or leaving the child with the family under court or child protective services supervision. Some states have statutes which provide that when the child is allowed to remain in the home after an adjudicatory finding of abuse or neglect, the parent is required to participate in a counseling program designated by the court or to conform with any other orders of the court.

Although juvenile court proceedings for child abuse or neglect vary throughout the United States, the Constitution guarantees the basic rights of due process which state courts must implement. Nevertheless, the content and procedure of abuse and neglect hearings remain relatively unsettled and procedural requirements and rights of parties differ from jurisdiction to jurisdiction.

(1) <u>Right to privacy</u>: Invasions of privacy may occur in a child abuse or neglect investigation when (a) questioning parents as to what particular sexual acts they perform in their marriage; seeking information from a parent's employer about his or her performance when the information has

no relevance to the investigation; and entering someone's house and looking through cabinets and drawers when no one is home.

Generally speaking, the criterion used to decide whether or not legal action can be brought for invasion of privacy is whether it would be highly objectionable to a reasonable person. For example, breaking into a house might be justifiable if there has been a report that a three-year-old has been abandoned with both legs broken.

Some invasions of privacy are not held actionable because the courts find an overriding public interest in obtaining the information. For example, some state statutes allow the child protective services worker to talk with a child without the parent's permission. Other states allow photographs of the child's injuries to be taken without parental permission.

(2) Proper notice of the proceeding: Parents must be given timely and substantive notice of abuse and/or neglect hearings so that they may address the allegations being made against them. The parents should receive a copy of the complaint or petition so that they are informed of the charges made. Notice requires that parents be informed that a hearing is to take place, when it will be held, and what the proposed subject matter will be. Notice must be provided to any person whose rights might be affected by the proceeding, whether or not they are respondents. Even in cases where the parents are not married, the U.S. Supreme Court has found that the father has a substantial interest at stake. It is not clear whether the child has the same right to notice as the parents.

(3) Right to a hearing: A hearing is required before a child can be removed from the home without parental consent, except in emergency situations. But if an emergency action is taken, a hearing must be held afterward. Some states allow for the removal of the child with parental consent alone. In these states, the parents may waive the right to a hearing for themselves and for the child as well.

(4) <u>Right to counsel</u> (guardian <u>ad litem</u>):
The right to counsel in juvenile proceedings
for parent and/or child varies on a state-to-state
basis.* Several courts have now held that right
to counsel in abuse and neglect proceedings is required by due process and equal protection of the
laws provisions of the Constitution. When the outcome of a delinquency hearing may be confinement
of the juvenile, counsel is mandatory. Some states
grant a general statutory right to counsel without
indicating the types of proceedings the statute
includes. Whether or not the right applies to other
delinquency hearings remain unclear under such
statutes.

Twenty jurisdictions require the appointment
of a guardian <u>ad litem</u> to represent the child, but
do not specify further qualifications for appointment. They are: Alaska, Arkansas, Colorado, Delaware, Georgia, Iowa, Maine, Minnesota, Mississippi,
Missouri, Nebraska, New Mexico, North Dakota, Ohio,
Rhode Island, South Carolina, Utah, American Samoa,
Puerto Rico, and the Virgin Islands.

Eleven other states expressly provide that
the guardian <u>ad litem</u> must be an attorney: Alabama,
District of Columbia, Florida, Idaho, Kansas, New
Jersey, New York, North Carolina, Pennsylvania,
Virginia, and Wisconsin.

Nine states require that legal counsel be
appointed to represent the child in abuse and neglect proceedings. They are: Arizona, California,
Connecticut, Michigan, Nevada, New Hampshire, Oklahoma, South Dakota, and West Virginia. At least

---

*Adapted from, <u>Representation for the Abused
and Neglected Child: Guardian Ad Litem and</u>
Legal Counsel, M. Alderman of Herner and
Company, for the National Center on Child
Abuse and Neglect, U.S. Department of Health
and Human Services, Washington, D.C. (1980).

one state, South Carolina, provides for the appointment of both a guardian _ad litem_ and legal counsel to represent the child.

Several states have specific conditions or requirements in their statutes providing for legal counsel or a guardian _ad litem_. For example, in Illinois, unless the guardian _ad litem_ is an attorney, the minor must be represented by counsel. In Vermont the court may appoint a guardian _ad litem_ or counsel. In Wyoming and Connecticut any attorney representing a child also serves as the child's guardian _ad litem_ unless a separate guardian _ad litem_ has been appointed by the court.

Only one state, Connecticut, further specifies the qualifications of the appointed representative. The Connecticut statute requires appointed counsel to be knowledgeable about the needs and protection of children.

A number of jurisdictions also specify in their legislation the persons who can and cannot serve as the representative for the child. Thus California provides that the probation officer or social worker who files the petition shall serve as the child's guardian _ad litem_. Tennessee law states that a party to the proceeding or his employee or representative shall not be appointed as the guardian _ad litem_ for the child. North Carolina prohibits the appointment of a public defender as guardian _ad litem_. Wisconsin law states that the guardian _ad litem_ shall not be the same as counsel for the alleged abuser or neglector or any governmental or social agency involved. South Carolina requires that counsel for the child shall in no case be the same as counsel for the parent, guardian, or other person subject to the proceeding or any governmental or social agency involved in the proceedings.

The right to representation created by state law may be either absolute or discretionary. Thirty-five jurisdictions require that a representative for the child be appointed in all abuse or neglect proceedings:

83

Alabama	New Jersey
Alaska	New Mexico
Arkansas	New York
California	North Dakota
Colorado	Ohio
Connecticut	Pennsylvania
District of Columbia	Rhode Island
Florida	Utah
Illinois	Virginia
Iowa	Washington
Kansas	West Virginia
Maine	Wisconsin
Massachusetts	Wyoming
Minnesota	American Samoa
Mississippi	Guam
Missouri	Puerto Rico
Nebraska	Virgin Islands
New Hampshire	

Sixteen other states have only discretionary statutes that empower but do not mandate courts to appoint a guardian ad litem or legal counsel when it appears to them that this would be in the child's best interests, or when otherwise needed to promote fairness and justice. They are: Arizona, Delaware, Georgia, Hawaii, Idaho, Indiana, Kentucky, Louisiana, Maryland, Montana, Nevada, North Carolina, Oklahoma, Oregon, Texas, and Vermont.

Only a few jurisdictions define in their statutes the duties and responsibilities of the appointed representative. North Carolina provides one of the most detailed descriptions of these responsibilities:

> The duties of the guardian ad litem shall be to make an investigation to determine the facts, the needs of the child, and the resources available within the family and in the community to meet those needs; to appear on behalf of the child in order to present the relevant facts to the court

84

at the adjudicatory part
of the hearing and at the
possible options to the
court at the disposition-
al part of the hearing; to
serve the child and the
court by protecting and
promoting the best interests
of and the least detrimental
alternatives for the child
at every stage of the proceeding until formally relieved of the responsibility by the court; to appeal,
when deemed advisable, from
an adjudication or order of
disposition to the Court
of Appeals...

- N.C. GEN. STAT. 7A-283

The Colorado statute also sets forth the
responsibilities of the guardian ad litem:

The guardian ad litem
shall be charged in
general with the representation of the child's
interests. To that end
he shall make such fur-
ther investigations as
he deems necessary to
ascertain the facts,
talk with or observe the
child involved, inter-
view witnesses and the
foster parents of the
child, and examine and
cross-examine witnesses
in both the adjudicatory
and dispositional hear-
ings and may introduce
and examine his own wit-
nesses, make recommen-
dations to the court con-
cerning the child's wel-

fare, and participate
further in the proceed-
ings to the degree nec-
essary to adequately
represent the child.

- COLO. REV. STAT. 19-10-
113(3)

Although few state legislatures define the
duties of the child's representative by statute,
these responsibilities may be found in the administrative regulations or be defined by judicial
decisions.

Ohio expresses in its law the responsibility
of the court to ensure effective representation
for the child:

The court shall require
such guardian ad litem
to faithfully discharge
his duties, and upon his
failure to do so shall
discharge him and appoint
another.

- OHIO REV. CODE ANN. 2151.
281

The appointment of the guardian ad litem is
intended to provide the child with independent
legal representation, and thus with protection
that could not be provided by attorneys representing the state or the parents.

The court may appoint the guardian ad litem
at any time in the hearing process, but it is generally accepted that he or she should be appointed
when the child first receives notice of legal proceedings or when the child's interests are first
threatened.

As an advocate for the child, the guardian
ad litem assumes four functions: (1) investigator

to discover all facts relevant to the case; (2) advocate to ensure that all relevant facts are brought before the court; (3) counsel to ensure that the court is aware of all dispositional options; (4) guardian to ensure that the child's interests are fully protected in court proceedings.

The guardian ad litem also serves as the child's spokesperson by allowing the child to express his or her own wishes and by presenting them to the court.

Parents may retain counsel on their own to represent them. However, if parents do not retain their own counsel, the court is not required to appoint or provide counsel for them from court funds unless this is mandated by state statute. Parents may always retain counsel for the child, but the court is required to appoint counsel only in those cases listed in the state codes.

(5) Right to a jury trial. A jury trial is not constitutionally required in a juvenile court. However, states by law may provide jury trials in juvenile hearings. A number of states do require them, either by statute or by judicial decision, usually upon request of one of the involved parties.

(6) Right of confrontation and cross-examination. In determining whether or not a party is entitled to the right of confrontation and cross-examination, the courts look at the potential seriousness of the impact of the hearing upon the individual, either parent or child. Given the gravity of a determination of abuse or neglect, and the repercussions such a finding may have upon parent or child, it would appear that all parties should be accorded this right. Of course, the effectiveness of this right depends upon representation by counsel.

To date, the United States Supreme Court has not held that a juvenile who is the subject of child abuse and/or neglect hearings has a right under the Sixth Amendment to confront and cross-examine witnesses. The states, by statute or by court decisions, may grant this right in such hearings. Generally it appears that when counsel is provided for the child, counsel is allowed to examine the witness. In addition, the right of parents to confront and cross-examine witnesses in child abuse and neglect hearings is based on the Sixth Amendment.

(7) Right to family integrity. Authority now exists in some jurisdictions to the effect that before a natural family relationship is terminated, attempts must be made to rehabilitate the family. Statutes in some states express a preference for care, guidance and control within the child's natural home. The court can put conditions on the child's remaining at home, such as cooperation with child protective services personnel, mandated counseling, or correctional therapy for the parents or family unit.

Chapter 4
PROOF AND EVIDENCE IN CHILD ABUSE
AND NEGLECT CASES*

In any child abuse and/or neglect hearing, reference to the jurisdiction's statute is essential. The statute is the source of the definition of child abuse and neglect. It also provides the guidelines or criteria of how much proof or how much information is necessary to persuade the court that the child is in need of protection.

Although standards of proof and rules of evidence apply to all types of child abuse and neglect hearings, they are most stringently applied in the adjudicatory hearing.

Standard of Proof

The burden of proof in any child abuse or neglect hearing is always on the petitioner. The standard of proof varies from jurisdiction to jurisdiction, and varies depending on the type of hearing.

In general, there are three standards of proof: beyond a reasonable doubt, clear and convincing evidence, and preponderance of the evidence.

The highest standard of proof required in United States courts is beyond a reasonable doubt which is applied in criminal proceedings and in all juvenile proceedings that could result in incarceration. The beyond a reasonable doubt test

---

*Source: Child Protection: The Role of the Courts, edited and produced by Kirschner Associates, Inc., under contract for the U.S. Department of Health and Human Services (Washington, D.C. 1980)

requires that the evidence point to one conclusion. It leaves no reasonable doubt about that conclusion.

But the standard of proof in child abuse and neglect hearings (normally the adjudicatory hearing) is usually either <u>clear and convincing evidence</u> (the intermediate test) or <u>preponderance of the evidence</u> (the test normally applied in civil proceedings).

Thirty-three states have required at least clear and convincing evidence in what is known as "termination of parental rights" proceedings when the issue is abuse. The remaining minority of states required only a preponderance of the evidence, meaning that after all the evidence has been weighed, the outcome will be in favor of the side that has presented the most convincing evidence. But in March, 1982, the United States Supreme Court ruled that a New York statute failed to give parents due process of law because it requires only a "fair preponderance of the evidence" to support the judicial finding of "permanent neglect," a term that also encompasses physical abuse. The Court stated that, "Before a State may sever completely and irrevocably the rights of parents in their natural child, due process requires that the State support its allegations by at least clear and convincing evidence" <u>Santosky v. Kramer</u> No. 80-5889.

The <u>best interests of the child</u> normally applies to custody determinations in separation or divorce proceedings. It is not a standard of proof, but rather a criterion for judicial disposition. It is used in the dispositional hearing after there has been a finding of abuse/neglect, as a basis for determining appropriate court orders. It is only sometimes applied in the adjudicatory hearing.

In many states, evidence at the fact-finding hearing must be:

> (1) <u>Competent</u>: It conforms to the legal rules of evidence.

     (2) <u>Material</u>: The facts prove
         the issue before the court;
         they have a direct bearing
         on the issue (whether the
         child is abused and/or ne-
         glected); or they have an
         effective influence or
         bearing at issue.

     (3) <u>Relevant</u>.

There are four kinds of evidence that qualify
as <u>competent</u> or conform to the rules of evidence:

     (1) <u>Direct evidence</u>: factual
         information without re-
         quiring the proof of any
         other facts, such as the
         witness's own conversa-
         tions with the parent and/
         or child, or the witness's
         own observations.

     (2) <u>Real or demonstrative ev-
         idence</u>: concrete evidence,
         such as a child in court
         with injuries, the instru-
         ment that caused the in-
         juries, X-rays or photo-
         graphs of the injuries.

     (3) <u>Circumstantial evidence</u>:
         direct observations that
         will permit the court to
         reach a specific conclusion.
         For example, if the parent
         had glazed eyes and slurred
         speech, was unable to stand
         or walk, and smelled of
         alcohol, the conclusion
         could be reached that the
         person was intoxicated.
         However, the witness may
         not testify that the parent
         was drunk, as this is a
         conclusion. Only direct

observations may be presented.

(4) Expert or opinion evidence:
evidence provided by a witness who has special expertise, skill or knowledge
which is beyond that of the
average person. Opinions
may be offered on the matter
at issue, for example, by
the pediatrician who diagnosed the child's injuries.

No consistent rules are followed by all states
for admissibility of evidence in juvenile court
proceedings. In some jurisdictions, a case may be
proven by any combination of these types of evidence, and in other jurisdictions by one type ex-
clusively if there is sufficient accumulation of
it. This means that, in some states, circumstantial
evidence may be sufficient for a court to take
jurisdiction. Rules vary from state to state but
are consistent within a particular state.

The rules of evidence exclude any evidence
which is "hearsay," that is, oral or written evidence which is not based on the witness's own
personal knowledge or observation but on something
said or written by someone other than the parties
before the court. An exception to this basic rule
is records kept in the course of business. The
objection to hearsay evidence is that it is not
subject to cross-examination.

Usually, certain conversations (such as those
between doctor and patient, clergy and penitent,
husband and wife, attorney and client) are recognized as "privileged" and absolutely confidential,
and therefore excluded from testimony. However,
in most states, direct statutory language, designed
to protect children subject to child abuse and/or
neglect, abrogates certain rights of privileged
conversation, such as that between doctor and
patient or husband and wife (see Table D). The
privileged communications between patient and
doctor have to be given careful consideration if

the patient is a child. To ascertain which **privileges** can and which cannot be claimed, it is essential to refer to the state's statutory **exceptions** and to the case law.

A preliminary or pretrial hearing is usually not bound by the legal rules of evidence. Hearsay is often admissible. At the dispositional hearing information may be considered that could not be admitted at the adjudicatory hearing. The most important information of this type is the predispositional investigation and social study. These reports usually do contain hearsay. Nevertheless, if the report is to be used by the court it must be accurate and complete, otherwise any disposition based on it will be open to legal challenge.

Use of Records

Records kept in the course of business are an exception to the hearsay rule and may be admitted as evidence. For a record to qualify as evidence, it must meet the following criteria:

(1) Entries were made in the regular course of business, and it is the practice to make and keep such records. For example, a hospital and child protective services agency usually qualify as businesses. Thus the transcribed notes of a child protective services worker qualify as do, of course, hospital records.

(2) Entries were made at, or reasonably close to, the time the event occurred. For example, if a child protective services worker makes an entry into the case record, describing from memory an event that occurred six months earlier,

the record does not qualify.
The judge determines whether
or not there was too long
a delay before entry into
the record. This determination is based on whether
the information is reliable,
considering the delay be-
fore the entry.

(3) Entries were made by someone who has personal knowledge of the facts, or en-
tries came from someone
who had the knowledge and
communicated that knowledge
to someone responsible
for making entries. This
may be subject to state
variation, particularly
if a state has adopted the
Federal Rules of Evidence
and Procedure which are
more liberal and do not
require testimony of a
witness to authenticate
the writing.

After a record is qualified, it becomes
primary and independent evidence. Thus, conclusions
such as "the house was filthy" are not sufficient
to stand alone. The record must describe the conditions in detail which lead to the conclusion
that the house was filthy.

In order to admit a record as evidence, a
witness who is familiar with the procedure for
creating the record is called. In his or her testimony, the witness must:

(1) identify the record;

(2) describe the method of preparing the record;

(3) state the time of preparation

94

     (4) testify that record-
        keeping is a part of
        the business of the
        office.

Use of Admissions

  Admissions can be offered as evidence in a
criminal case against the defendant except when
illegally obtained. An admission is not always a
confession. However, a guilty plea to a criminal
charge can be used against that person in a later
court action involving the same situation. For
example, although it is considered hearsay in a
later court action, a guilty plea to criminal
child abuse may be offered as evidence in a subsequent juvenile court hearing to determine jurisdiction over a child or in a hearing on termination
of parental rights. The plea, however, would not
be sufficient grounds to make a finding of abuse/
neglect.

  Furthermore, admissions can be used as evidence in a juvenile court hearing, for example,
when a parent acknowledges to the child protective
services worker or other responsible professional
that he or she abused the child. The parent's admission is allowed as evidence to prove the act
and can be used in any subsequent hearing. This
demonstrates the importance of keeping accurate
and timely records of all conversations relevant
to the case by those who are working on it.

How to Prove Child Maltreatment*

  When attempting to prove a civil court case
of child abuse and neglect, the need to protect
the child against the actions or failures to act
on the part of his/her parents or caretakers must
be shown. The need for protection, although not
observable, may be inferred from present circumstances which are observable. A showing that harm
is likely to occur to the child indicates to the

---

*Based on material developed by D.J. Beshariv

court the child's need for protection. The court's action is justified by the need to provide protection for the child.

For example, harm may be proven in a case where a three-month old child was admitted to the hospital with a spiral fracture and several other fractures in different stages of healing. The parents' explanation of the current fracture did not correspond with the actual injury incurred. In addition, it was determined during the investigation that the parents had been married only for one year and had recently moved into the city and that there had been a prior substantiated report of abuse in another city.

There are six elements of proof which, while all not applicable in each case, must be offered to prove a case of child abuse and neglect:

      (1) The child

      (2) The actual harm to the child

      (3) The act or omission causing harm

      (4) The act or omission attempting harm or having potential for harm

      (5) Endangerment or inferred harm

      (6) The person(s) responsible

The two essential elements which must be shown in any child abuse and neglect hearing are the vulnerability of the child and the person responsible.

(1) The child: A determination of the vulnerability of the child includes a review of such factors as the child's age, sex, developmental status and special characteristics. For example, an infant, a physically handicapped child, or a mentally retarded child is less able to defend

96

himself or herself from abuse than a seventeen-year-old "normal" child.

(2) The person(s) responsible: The assessment of the person responsible for the act(s) or omission(s) causing harm or attempting or having the potential for harm must include consideration of a number of factors.

A. The relationship to the child: Whether the perpetrator is in the home infrequently or is the primary caretaker has a direct bearing on the child's need for the court's protection. For example, abuse of the child is more likely to recur in a situation where the person responsible is the primary caretaker of the child by virtue of the fact that the person is with the child consistently and there is thus more time for abuse to occur.

B. Relevant past behaviors: It is important to consider past behaviors of the caretaker which are related to the child's need for protection. For example, the parent has previously abused another child. Or the parent has had frequent hospitalizations for severe psychiatric problems. Or the parent has been hospitalized for alcohol or drug related problems.

C. Internal and external conditions: The external and internal factors affecting the caretaker's behavior should be considered when attempting to determine predictable future harm to the child. These include:

(i) the occurrence, duration, and kind of stress;

            (ii) the availability of external
                 supports;

            (iii) the strengths and problems
                  of the caretaker.

    D. Predictable future behavior: It
       is important to demonstrate the
       likelihood that parents will be-
       have in a harmful or potentially
       harmful manner in the future. Such
       a demonstration depends on the
       assessment of the relationship
       of the person responsible to the
       child, the relevant past behaviors,
       and/or the internal and external
       conditions.

    3. Actual harm to the child. Actual harm is
a harm that is present now. It may be known through
observation of physical or behavioral indicators
in the child. Harm in the form of a physical injury, such as lateral bruises on the buttocks or
multiple fractures in a child under two years of
age, can be observed by any professional. An
emotional harm may be exhibited through the unusual or maladaptive behaviors of the child. For
example, a child may engage in self-destructive
behavior such as biting himself and head-banging,
or may appear extremely withdrawn or aggressive.

    There are three essential factors in proving
actual harm to the child which must be presented
in a child abuse and neglect hearing in order to
show that the child is in need of protection (that
is, prediction of future harm).

            A. Indicators of abuse/neglect:
               The physical and/or behavioral
               indicators in an abused/neglected
               child must be assessed and offered
               as evidence during a court hearing.
               Physical indicators may include:
               large areas of bruises on the child's
               torso, back, or thighs; unexplained
               spiral fractures; abnormal hemogoblin

98

count; abnormally low weight. Behavorial
indicators may include: obsessive or
compulsive behavior in a child; developmental delays; fear of physical contact
with parents or other adults; constant
fatigue; listlessness or hunger.

In cases where there are physical indicators of abuse/neglect in the child,
it is preferable to present photographs
or X-rays (if appropriate) of the child's
injuries. Expert medical testimony is
frequently necessary to prove actual
physical harm to the child. Expert
witnesses may also present evidence
based on psychological or developmental
evaluations or testing.

B. Severity: The severity of the harm
to the child must be assessed and
offered in a child abuse and neglect
court hearing. The degree of injury
to the child is the measurement used
in assessing the severity of actual
harm. For example, any fracture, lacerations which require extensive sutures,
or second and/or third degree burns
on the child's body would be considered
serious injuries. A fractured skull
is more serious in nature than a black
eye and would tend to prove the severity
of the harm to the child. A mild de-
pression in an emotional abuse case
is less serious than a psychosis.

C. Present suffering and future dysfunction:
The third interrelated factor to be
assessed is the nature of the child's
present suffering and/or future dysfunction. The questions to be asked
are: "How is the harm to the child
affecting his or her present functioning?" and "What is the probability
and extent of future dysfunction?"

(4) Act or omission causing harm: A showing

of actual harm to the child is insufficient to prove a case of child maltreatment. It is also necessary to show an act or omission by the child's caretaker (person responsible), causing the harm. For example, it must be shown that the child's delays in development were caused by severe and continuous lack of emotional and physical stimulation.

A. Type of act or omission (abuse/neglect): The type of abuse/neglect must also be presented as evidence when attempting to prove that an act or omission resulted in harm to the child. The following is a partial categorization of the types of acts or omissions:

(i) sexual abuse
(ii) physical abuse
(iii) emotional abuse
(iv) failure to meet the child's nutritional needs
(v) failure to provide for physical shelter from the elements
(vi) failure to protect a child from dangers in the environment if protection is within the parent's control
(vii) failure to meet the child's health needs, including specific medical care
(viii) failure to meet the child's emotional needs
(ix) failure to meet the child's intellectual needs
(x) failure to provide the child with moral guidance and supervision

In addition, some acts or omissions are by their nature more serious because of their greater potential for harm. For example, the use of a knife resulting in injury to the child would be more serious than the use of a hand resulting in a bruise. The nature of acts or omissions, while varying considerably, is important when presenting evidence, in order to prove that the child is in need of protection.

B. Chronicity: The chronicity, that is the number and duration of the acts or missions in causing harm in the identified child and other children in the same care, must be assessed. This is particularly important in emotional abuse cases. For example, one instance of a parent verbally degrading and humiliating a child would not substantiate a case, but the establishment of a pattern of similar instances would, and thus would reinforce the need for court action to protect the child.

C. Multiplicity: If there is a variety of acts or omissions resulting in harm to the identified child or other children under the same care, the need for court-ordered protection of the child will be strengthened. For example, a case where a six-year-old child is expected to care for her eight-month-old sister for extended periods of time, is not allowed outside to play with friends, and is disciplined by being made to stand in the corner for two hours at a time.

D. Reasons for the act(s) or omission(s): The level of responsibility of the perpetrator is an essential element in proving to the court that the child is in need of protection. There are three levels of responsibility:

(i) Willful: Those situations where the harm is consciously intended;

(ii) Reckless: Those situations where the harm is the result

of a disregard of a known
risk or danger of harm;

(iii) Negligent: Those situations
where harm is the result of
a disregard of risk or danger
that would have been deemed
hazardous by most "reasonable"
persons, although it is not
recognized as hazardous by
the perpetrator.

E. Mitigating or excusing conditions:
Mitigating or excusing conditions
which may affect the court's decision
about a caretaker's behavior regardless of the level of responsibility,
must be considered when preparing
and presenting a child abuse and
neglect case in court. Although the
following mitigating conditions may
be thought to justify the caretaker's
behavior, the presence of any of these
conditions does not necessarily elim-
inate the need for court action.

(i) Parental privileges: To discipline a child, either physically
or by withholding privileges;

(ii) Choice of evils: To choose the
lesser of two evils. For example, a seven-year-old child
is engaging in self-destructive
behavior and the only way his
parents can prevent him from
harming himself is to physically restrain him;

(iii) Protection of personal property; may be an issue in case
of adolescent abuse;

(iv) Provocation and self-defense:
usually only an issue in adolescent abuse cases;

(v) <u>Mistake</u>: In law or in fact.

(5) <u>Endangered or inferred harm</u>: Since there is not yet any observable harm to the child, it becomes necessary to prove that the child in fact suffered harm as the inevitable result of the act(s) or omission(s) of the person(s) responsible. It is almost always necessary to have expert witnesses provide testimony to support this conclusion. For example, it can be assumed that an infant who has consistently received little if any physical and emotional stimulation has suffered harm that may result in serious developmental delays; or a four-year-old child who is continuously belittled by his or her parents and who, unlike his or her siblings, is the recipient of excessive discipline, has suffered harm which will be manifested through psychological difficulties. In both of these cases it is essential to provide expert testimony by professionals such as a pediatrician or child psychiatrist, which will tend to prove inferred harm to the child.

Chapter 5
CHILD SEXUAL ABUSE*

Child sexual abuse is a crime in every jurisdiction. The term "sexual abuse of children" encompasses a wide range of acts committed against minors. It may be defined in a state criminal code by incest or sex crimes statutes. A separate definition may appear in state child abuse reporting laws or juvenile court acts. It may encompass sexual acts perpetrated by family members or persons in a position of authority over the child, as well as acts by acquaintances and strangers. For the purpose of this discussion, however, sexual abuse is here defined to include any contacts or interactions between a child and other family members in a position of power or control over the child, where the child is being used for the sexual stimulation of the perpetrator or another person.

Background and Incidence

In 1912, Kraft-Ebing introduced the term "pedophilla erotica." This label describes behavior which manifests itself in abnormal erotic sexual abuse of pre-adolescent children. More recently, however, some authorities suggest that sexual abuse by a family member is more likely to be symptomatic of family dysfunction rather than a primary sexual orientation toward children. There are certain

---

*Sources: Child Sexual Abuse: Legal Issues and Approaches, monograph of the National Legal Resource Center for Child Advocacy and Protection, American Bar Association, Washington, D.C. (1980); Child Sexual Abuse and the Law, Report of the ABA National Legal Resource Center for Child Advocacy and Protection, Washington, D.C. (1981)

105

characteristics which child sex offenders often
share in common. These include isolation or alien-
ation from others, dysfunctional interpersonal
relationships, poor self-concepts, and lack of
impulse control. Most adults who commit sexual
offenses against children suffer from a personal-
ity disorder, but are not considered mentally
ill or psychotic. Furthermore, contrary to one
myth regarding perpetrators of child sex crimes,
the offender comes from a range of socio-economic
and educational backgrounds.

Incest has, of course, been a "taboo" in most
cultures throughout recorded history, evoking
severe social and legal sanctions. Yet, contrary
to popular belief, it is not as rare a phenomenon
as once thought. It has been called "the crime
no one believes," since most people are uncomfort-
able even hearing about it, let alone talking
about it.

The actual incidence of child sexual abuse is
difficult to measure, since it is the most under-
reported form of child abuse. Until recently, it
was not even specifically covered by many state
mandatory child abuse reporting laws, although
most jurisdictions now include "sexual" abuse in
their reporting statutes. When reported, it has
generally been to law enforcement agencies which
do not necessarily relay this information to the
agency keeping child abuse reporting statistics.
Recent estimated figures have placed the incidence
of sexual abuse at 800 to 1,000 cases per million
population or a rate of over 200,000 children per
year.

In 1978, 15.4% of all children for whom reports
of abuse were substantiated were found to be sexually abused. The victims of sexual abuse are both
girls and boys, although there is a much higher
rate of girls who are reported as sexually abused
than boys. There is, however, an increase in boy-
victims being seen by treatment programs. Although
the average age of the child is between 11 and 14,
treatment programs report seeing children as young
as 2 or 3, some of whom are detected because they

have contracted gonorrhea. In a large percentage
of incest cases, the offense is repeated over a
period of time ranging from weeks to several
years. There is rarely an application of force or
threat of bodily harm, and more often the child is
psychologically enticed by loyalty to, affection with
with, and dependence upon the adult caretaker.

Sexual Abuse in Juvenile/Family Court Jurisdiction Acts

All states have established statutory standards, criteria, and procedures for bringing a
civil child protective proceeding in the juvenile
or family court based on an allegation of abuse by
a parent or caretaker. Most states have specific
statutory provisions defining an abused and neglected child for purposes of juvenile or family
court jurisdiction. Some states have separate
definitional provisions for abuse and neglect,
while others include abuse as part of their neglect definition. Some states refer to both abused
and neglected children as "dependent" or "in need
of care, supervision, or assistance," or by other
similar terms. For example: "child in need of
care....,"La. Rev. Stat. Ann. art. 13 (Supp. 1980);
"child in need of assistance....," Pa. Stat. Ann.
tit. 42, Section6302 (Supp. 1979); "dependent
child....," R.I. Gen. Laws Section 14-1-3(h)
(Supp. 1979).

Like other types of child abuse, sexual abuse
may be the grounds for a child protection proceeding. Every state's statutory definitions can
be interpreted to include sexual abuse, even if
it is not explicitly mentioned. Many statutory
definitions of abuse and neglect utilize broad
and subjective language and fail to delineate
the specific harms from which children should be
protected by the court. For example, a number of
states define an abused or neglected child as a
child who "lacks proper parental care or control"
or whose "environment is injurious to the child's
health or welfare." This language could be interpreted to encompass sexual abuse. In seven states,
sexual abuse may be covered by language which is

107

not only broad, but tends to be somewhat inflam-
matory and even demeaning. In these states, an
abused or neglected child is defined in part as
one "whose home, by reason of neglect, cruelty,
drunkeness, immorality or depravity, on the part
of his parent, is an unfit or improper place."
States which carry such statutory definitions
include Alabama, Arizona, Arkansas, Michigan,
Oregon, Rhode Island, and Tennessee.

At least 21 states, plus American Samoa,
Guam, and the District of Columbia, have now
specifically included sexual abuse in their
jurisdictional definitions of abuse and/or neglect.
The 21 states are: Alaska, Connecticut, Florida,
Idaho, Indiana, Kansas, Kentucky, Louisiana,
Maine, Massachusetts, Mississippi, Montana, New
Jersey, New Mexico, New York, North Carolina,
Ohio, Virginia, Washington, West Virginia, and
Wisconsin. This legislative trend is part of an
overall movement toward defining with particular-
ity what abusive or neglectful acts should trigger
legal intervention to protect a child. While the
inclusion of sexual abuse in these provisions
is a positive step toward acknowledging this type
of child abuse, most statutes do not state what
acts constitute "sexual abuse." Only one state,
Kansas, defines the term "sexual abuse" as engaging in sexual intercourse or "any lewd fon-
dling or touching of the person of either the
minor or the defendant..." by a household or
family member with a child. Kan. Stat. Ann. Section 60-3102(A), (C) (Supp. 1979).

The juvenile court jurisdiction statutes in
New York, North Carolina, Ohio, Virginia, and
American Samoa define sexual abuse by reference
to their criminal sexual offense provisions. In
addition, New York's provision, which refers to
the penal law's definition, states that the
corroboration requirement in criminal cases involving sexual abuse of a child does not apply
to family court proceedings. Ohio's provision
states that the sexual activity must constitute
an offense under its criminal provisions, but
that the conviction of a sexual offense is not

necessary for a finding in the juvenile court
that a child has been sexually abused. Kentucky
and Washington specifically refer to the definitions in their child abuse and neglect reporting
statutes. A few other states have one definition
which applies to juvenile/family court proceedings
as well as to their reporting procedures: Indiana,
Montana, New Mexico, and West Virginia are examples of such states. These states have generally
amended their codes by combining under one chapter
all the statutory provisions relating to abused
and neglected children, and in some states, delinquent children.

In all jurisdictions, if one parent is abusive
and the other fails to prevent the abuse from
occurring, a child protection proceeding may be
brought against the passive parent as well as the
abusive parent. In this situation, the passive
parent would be considered responsible for allowing the abuse to occur (i.e., failing to properly
care for and protect the child). Thus, neglect
statutes with language such as "lacks proper
parental control and care" may be interpreted to
cover parents who have knowingly (or unknowingly)
allowed their children to be victims of sexual
abuse within the home. Nine statutes clearly
establish juvenile/family court jurisdiction over
the passive parent in a sexual abuse situation;
they define such a parent as one who "allows the
sexual abuse to be committed," or by other similar
language: Alaska Stat. Section 47.10.010(2)(D)
(1979); Ky. Rev. Stat. Section 199.011(6) (Supp.
1978); Mont. Rev. Codes Ann. Section 41-3-100
(Supp. 1979); N.J. Stat. Ann. Section 9:6-8.21(C)
(3)(Supp. 1980); N.Y. Fam. Ct. Act Section 1012(E)
(III) (McKinney Supp. 1978); N.C. Gen. Stat. Section 7A-517(I)(C)(Supp. 1979); Va. Code Section
16.1-228(A)(4) Supp.1979); W. Va. Code Ann. Section 49-1-3 (Supp. 1979). D.C. Code Section 16-
2301 (9)(1978).

In the majority of child sexual abuse cases,
the father is the abusive parent. In such cases,
the culpability of the mother becomes a significant issue in considering first, whether to ini-

tiate a juvenile court proceeding against both parents, and second, whether the child should be removed from the mother's custody. The mother's knowledge of the sexual abuse is important in deciding whether a child neglect proceeding against her would be appropriate. Much of the sociological and psychological literature dealing with incest dynamics indicates that the mother often unconsciously condones the sexual abuse and may feel divided loyalty between the father and the child. On the other hand, the mother may assert that she had no knowledge of the abuse and may be willing to protect the child from further harm. Where this is the case, and where the father has agreed to move or been forced out of the home (or has been incarcerated), a juvenile court proceeding against the non-abusive mother may not be appropriate. Nonetheless, there may be situations in which the abuser is out of the home, but where a proceeding against the mother is advisable. In such cases, removal of the child from the mother's home might not be the recommended disposition; instead, for example, juvenile court action may be needed to insure, through protective supervision, that the child and mother are obtaining treatment.

Domestic Violence Statutes

In recent years, a new remedy has emerged through which children (particularly with supportive mothers) can obtain a civil protective order to prevent further sexual abuse committed by a perpetrator within the family. Although these laws were designed principally to provide a remedy for battered women, many have language allowing any "family member," or someone acting on a child's behalf, to petition a court for a protective order because of an abusive act committed by any member of the household (not just a parent or relative). There are at present 34 states which have such statutes. In eight states, the law specifically provides a remedy for sexually abused children, while other state laws might be interpreted to provide such remedy. The states with statutes protecting sexually abused children are: Delaware, Kansas, Maryland, Massachusetts, Minnesota, Oregon, Pennsylvania, and West Virginia.

Under these laws, orders can be sought to have the sexually abused household member (parent, mother's boyfriend, etc.) vacate the family home. This places the "get out of the house" sanction, where its use is appropriate, on the abuser and not on the child. Under traditional child protective laws, juvenile court judges lack the authority to remove an adult perpetrator from the home. These new legal remedies therefore provide a quick means of protecting a child and her cooperative mother from all forms of violence (including the sometimes co-existent battering of the mother). A mother may want the abuser out of the house but not criminally convicted and sentenced. She may also be more willing to cooperate with the authorities in these cases, since she does not want to risk the loss of her child.

Some of the domestic violence statutes also have special provisions relating to dispositions in criminal proceedings involving intra-familial abuse. For example, the Massachusetts' statute explicitly states that whenever a criminal complaint is issued for intra-familial abuse, including sexual abuse, a court may impose as a condition of the defendant's pre-trial release "such terms as will insure the safety of the person... and will prevent its recurrence. Such terms shall include reasonable restrictions on the travel, association or place of abode of the defendant as will prevent such person from contact with the person abused." Similar terms may be imposed as a condition of probation. In addition, the statute specifically allows referral of the defendant for treatment a condition of disposition or probation.

In most jurisdictions, courts possess discretion in criminal cases to order a variety of conditions to pre-trial release or probation. However, specific statutory authorizing encourages courts to impose terms such as ordering the defendant to vacate the home. This kind of approach in a criminal proceeding would make it unnecessary for the juvenile court to remove the child from the home where the mother is able to care for and protect the child.

Evidentiary Problems

The threshold question in all child abuse cases relates to the competency of the child victim/witness. Most jurisdictions no longer set an age below which a child is incompetent to testify. Instead, the court has discretion to allow a child to testify if he or she is capable of accurately observing and communicating past events and understands the necessity of telling the truth (whether or not the abstract concept of an oath is comprehended). Children as young as three years have been held competent to testify if he or she is capable of accurately observing and communicating past events and understands the necessity of telling the truth (whether or not the abstract concept of an oath is comprehended). Children as young as three years have been held competent to testify in child sexual abuse cases.

Another important related issue is whether the child has fabricated the allegation of sexual molestation. Until recently, many psychiatrists trained in Freudian analysis, discounted children's reports of sexual attacks and attributed them to fantasy. The law's response to the perceived danger of false charges was to require corroboration of the child witness' testimony in sex offense cases. Current psychiatric theories, however, refuse the notion that children's detailed complaints of sexual assaults are fantasized. Many states now recognize this fact and have eliminated the requirement of corroboration for both minor as well as adult victims of sexual assault. Only four jurisdictions, the District of Columbia, Georgia, Nebraska, and New York, still require corroboration in all sex offense cases involving minors, although 17 states require corroboration of a child victim's testimony in special or limited circumstances. Twenty-

nine states have abolished a corroboration requirement in all sexual offense cases. Two jurisdictions, the District of Columbia and New York,
have eliminated the requirement for adult victims,
but retained it for child victims.

In cases of intra-familial abuse, the corroboration requirement may be of particularly
difficult impediment to prosecution. There is
usually no medical evidence to corroborate the
crime. Children who are victims of sexual abuse
by a parent or adult family member are rarely
forcibly assaulted. They are more often bribed
or cajoled. In addition, intra-familial sexual
abuse of children may involve sexual contact
short of penetration. Also, reports by a child
that he or she has been sexually abused, often
are made long past the time any physical evidence
might have existed.

But even where a strict corroboration requirement has been abolished, corroboration may be
necessary for a number of reasons. Juries are
less likely to convict on the basis of the child's
testimony alone, and defendants may be less in-
clined to plead guilty. Perhaps the greatest
hurdle in proving these cases, however, is not
so much the lack of corroboration as the fact
that the only available evidence is usually
circumstantial.

An important source of evidence is the medical
examination. In all cases of child sexual abuse
in which a medical examination is warranted
(usually where the sexual offense occurred very
recently), the child should be thoroughly exam-
ined, preferably by an experienced physician. In
addition to any physical evidence, the doctor
should also record a factual description of the
child's general appearance and emotional state.
The examination should be conducted with a view
toward utilizing the medical records and tests
as evidence in a trial. Statements made by the
child to the examining physician may be admissible
if they concern present pain or the cause of the
condition, where the cause is relevant to the

medical treatment or diagnosis. The medical records should be admissible at trial as a business records exception to the hearsay rule.

Other forms of evidence to prove abuse may include admissions by the defendant, evidence of prior similar offenses, evidence of opportunity for the abuse to have occurred, former testimony in civil proceedings, res gestae, or excited utterances by the child, and prior inconsistent statements. Many jurisdictions liberally construe what constitutes an excited utterance when made by a child abuse victim. Moreover, excited utterances of the child may be admissible even where the child would be incompetent to testify.

Another significant impediment to the successful prosecution of these cases is the risk that the child will change the story he or she gave earlier. Child victims of sexual abuse are frequently influenced or pressured by the perpetrator and other family members to recant their story. It is not unlikely for the child to later deny the incident since the abuse probably ceased as soon as court proceedings were initiated and he/she wants life to go back to normal. In most jurisdictions, prior inconsistent statements are admissible only to impeach the child's credibility. Prosecution may thus be unsuccessful if the child's trial testimony refutes the abuse. Therefore, as allowed in some states, a child's prior inconsistent statements should be admissible as substantive evidence.

Another traditional evidentiary problem which has been resolved in most states involves the husband-wife privilege. At common law, the husband-wife privilege actually included two separate privileges. One is called the "testimonial" privilege, in which a spouse who is a party in a legal action may prevent the other spouse from testifying for or against him or her. In child abuse cases, this privilege frequently becomes an issue when a spouse seeks to prevent adverse testimony by the other spouse. The second privilege involves confidential communications for exempting use of the marital privilege in child abuse cases. First, the customary purpose for the privilege, that of preserving family harmony, is no longer relevant when such harmony has already been disrupted by parental child abuse. Family solidarity should not be maintained at the expense of harm to the child. Second, there is a substantial need for the testimony of the mother or other spouse in these cases where other evidence is lacking or insufficient.

Most states have abrogated the adverse testimonial privilege in all judicial proceedings. In all except one state, Utah, this privilege has been abolished either in all criminal proceedings or in criminal cases involving child abuse and neglect. The communications privilege has not been abrogated in criminal cases or criminal cases involving child abuse or neglect in the following eight jurisdictions: District of Columbia, Georgia, Iowa, Maryland, Massachusetts, Mississippi, Montana, New Jersey, and Vermont. In civil cases, the communications privilege may still be invoked in child abuse or neglect cases in nine states: Georgia, Iowa, Maryland, Mississippi, Montana, New Jersey, Utah, Vermont, and Washington.*

---

*Note: Josephine Bulkley is to be credited for this material cited supra.

115

BIBLIOGRAPHY

Abandonment of Children As a Civil Wrong. Ohio
St. L.J. 41:533-52 (1980).

Absolute Liability or Not? R.L. Waters. Sol. J.
125:140-2 (1981).

Accountability in the Child Protection System: A
Defense of the Proposed Standards Relating to
Abuse and Neglect. R.R. McCathren, BU L. Rev.
57:707-31 (1977).

Alternative to the Judicial Process: Court Avoid-
ance in Child Neglect Cases. D. Cruickshank,
UBC L. Rev. 12:248-75 (1978).

Battered Child. R.H. Brown, Med. Tr. T.Q. 20:273-
81 (1974).

Battered Child Syndrome. J.A. Ramsey, B.J. Lawler,
Pepperdine L. Rev. 1:372-81 (1974).

Better Protection for the Defenseless- Tennessee's
Revised Mandatory Child Abuse Reporting Statute.
Memphis St. U.L. Rev. 4:585-93 (1974).

Care Proceedings: A Question of Priorities. B.
Hoggett, Sol. J. 120:727-9 (1976).

Case of Neglect: Parens Patriae versus Due Process
in Child Neglect Proceedings. Ariz. L. Rev. 17:
1055-89 (1975).

Case Study of Child Abuse: A Former Prosecutor's
View. J.J. McKenna, Am. Crim. L. Rev. 12:165-78
(1974).

Child Abuse and the Law: A Mandate for Change.

How. L.J. 18:200-19 (1973).

Child Abuse and the Law: The California System.
G.S. Goodpaster, K. Angel. Hastings L.J. 26:
1081-125 (1975).

Child Abuse: Attempts to Secure the Problem by
Reporting Laws. R.H. Brown. Women Law J. 60:73-
8 (1974).

Child Abuse and Maltreatment: The Development of
New York's Child Protection Laws. Fordham Urban
L.J. 5:533-47 (1977).

Child Abuse and Neglect: Historical Overview,
Legal Matrix and Social Perspectives on North
Carolina. M.P. Thomas, Jr. NC L. Rev. 51:293;
54:743-76 (1976).

Child Abuse and Neglect in North Dakota. W.N.
Friedrich, J.A. Boriskin. ND L. Rev. 51:197-224
(1976).

Child Abuse and Neglect Reporting Legislation in
Missouri. K.M. Krause, Mo. L. Rev. 42:207-31
(1977).

Child Abuse and Neglect: The Legal Challenge. G.
J. Pierron, J. Kan. BA 46:167-81 (1977).

Child Abuse and the Law in Massachusetts: In
Search of a Proper Defendant. New England L.Rev.
13:802-34 (1978).

Child Abuse Symposium: Introductory comments.
W.F. Mondale; A glance at the past, a gaze at
the present, a glimpse of the future: a critical
analysis of the development of child abuse reporting statutes. B.G. Fraser; Putting central
registers to work: using modern management information systems to improve child protective
services. D.J. Besharov; Civil liability in
child abuse cases. R.H. Brown, R.B. Truitt; The
role of attorneys on child abuse teams, R. Bourne;
Child abuse in the Netherlands: The medical
referee. J.E. Doek. Chi-Kent L. Rev. 54:635-826

(1978).

Child Abuse Reporting Statutes: The Case for holding Physicians civilly Liable for Failing to
Report. L.B. Isaacson. San Diego L. Rev. 12:743-
77 (1977).

Child Abuse: The Role of Adoption As a Preventive
Measure. John Marshall L.J. 10:546-66 (1977).

Child Abuse: Tomorrow's Problems Begin Today.
V.J. Fontana. Catholic Law 22: 297-304 (1976).

Child Abuse Victims: Are They Also Victims of an
Adversarial and Hierarchal Court System? Pepperdine L. Rev. 5:717-39 (1978).

Child Pornography: A New Role for the Obscenity
Doctrine. U. Ill. L.F. 1978:711-57 (1978).

Child's Emotional Health- The Need for Legal
Protection. Tulsa L.J. 15:299-326 (1979).

Child's Maltreatment: An Overview of Current
Approaches. J. Family L.J. 18:115-45 (1979).

Civil Liability for Failing to Report Child
Abuse. Det. Coll. L. Rev. 1977:135-66 (1977).

Commonwealth v. Cadwell (Mass.) 372 N.E. 2d 246:
Deliberate Premeditation, Extreme Atrocity and
Cruelty, and the Battered Child Syndrome- A
New Look At Criminal Culpability in Massachu-
setts. New England L. Rev. 14:812-47 (1979).

Connecticut's Child Abuse Law. E.R. Bard. Conn.
B.J. 48:260-78 (1974).

Constitutional Law-Due Process- Indigent Parents'
Rights to Counsel in Child Neglect Cases. Tenn.
L. Rev. 46:649-70 (1979).

Courts: Seen and Not Heard. The Child's Need for
His Own Lawyer in Child Abuse and Neglect Cases.
Okla L. Rev. 29:439-45 (1976).

Dependency Proceedings: What Standard of Proof?
An Argument Against the Standard of "Clear and
Convincing." San Diego L. Rev. 14:1155-75 (1977).

Dependency and Termination Proceedings in Califor-
nia- Standards of Proof. Hastings L. J. 30:1815-
41 (1979).

Domestic Violence Continuum: A Pressing Need for
Legal Intervention. F.G. Bolton, Jr. Women Law
J. 66:11-17 (1980).

Due Process and the Fundamental Right to Family
Integrity: A Re-evaluation of South Dakota's
Parental Termination Statute. SD L. Rev. 24:
447-65 (1979).

Due Process for Parents in Emergency Protection
Proceedings Under the Texas Family Code. Houston
L. Rev. 15:709-34 (1978).

Drug-Addicted Parents and Child Abuse. J. Densen-
Gerber, C.C. Rohrs. Contemp. Drug 2:683-95
(1973).

Evidence-Child Abuse- Expert Medical Testimony
Concerning "Battered Child Syndrome" Held
Admissible. Fordham L. Rev. 42:935-42 (1974).

Evidence- Marital Privilege Exception Expanded
to Include One Spouse's Testimony Against Other
in Federal Child Abuse Prosecutions. Cumb. L.
Rev. 7:177-84 (1976).

Evidentiary Problems in Criminal Child Abuse
Prosecutions. Geo. L.J. 63:257-73 (1974).

Evidentiary Problems of Proof in Child Abuses;
Why Family and Juvenile Courts Fail. J. Family
L. 13:818-52 (1973-4).

"Family Autonomy" or "Coercive Intervention"?
Ambiguity and Conflict in the Proposed Standards
for Child Abuse and Neglect. R. Bourbe. E.H.

Newberger, BU L. Rev. 57:670-706 (1977).

Family Law- Parental Rights- Principles of res
ipsa loquitur Apply to Proof of Child Abuse and
  Neglect. Tex. Tech. L. Rev. 9:335-42 (1977-8).

In the Child's Best Interests: Rights of the
  Natural Parents in Child Placement Proceedings.
  NYU L. Rev. 51:446-77 (1976).

Incest and Drug-Related Child Abuse- Systematic
  Neglect by the Medical and Legal Professions.
  J. Densen-Gerber, S.F. Hutchinson, R.M. Levine.
  Contemp. Drug 6:135-72 (1977).

Incest As a Causative Factor in Antisocial Behavior: An Exploratory Study. J. Benward, J.
  Densen-Gerber. Contemp. Drug 4:323-40 (1975).

Independent Representation for the Abused and
  Neglected Child; The Guardian ad liem. B.G.
  Fraser. Calif. Western L. Rev. 13:16-45 (1976-
  1977).

Indiana's Statutory Protection for the Abused
  Child. Val. U.L. Rev. 9:89-133 (1974).

Intervention Between Parent and Child: A Reappraisal of the State's Role in Child Abuse and
  Neglect Cases. J. Arleen. Geo. L. J. 63:887-
  937 (1975).

Iowa Professionals and the Child Abuse Reporting
  Statute- A Case of Success. Iowa L. Rev. 65:1273-
  385 (1980).

In Re Hofbauer (NY) 393 NE 2d 1009: May Parents
  Choose Unorthodox Care for Their Child? Albany
  L. Rev. 44:818-48 (1980).

Indiana's Approach to Child Abuse and Neglect: A
  Frustration of Family Integrity. H.E. Martz,
  Val. U. L. Rev. 14:69-121 (1979).

Judge v. Social Worker: Can Arbitrary Decision-making Be Tempered By the Courts? M.R. Lowry. NYU L. Rev. 52:1033-50 (1977).

Lawyers, Psychologists, and Psychological Evidence in Child Protection Hearings. J.R. Groves. Queen's L.J. 5:241-68 (1980).

Legal Advocacy for the Maltreated Child. D.C. Bross. Trial 14:29-32 (1978).

Legal Research on Child Abuse and Neglect: Past and Future. Family L. Q. 11:51-84 (1977).

Legal Responses to Child Abuse. B.M. Dickens. Family L.Q. 12:1-36 (1978).

Malpractice Liability for Failing to Report Child Abuse. R.J. Kohlman, Calif. S. BJ 49:118-23 (1974).

Medical & Legal Aspects of the Battered Child Syndrome. R.H. Brown, Chi.-Kent L. Rev. 50:45-84 (1973).

Maryland Laws on Child Abuse and Neglect: History, Analysis, and Reform. U. Balt. L. Rev. 6:113-36 (1976).

Medical, Legislative, and Legal Aspects of Child Abuse and Neglect: A Symposium. Preface. The Maltreated Children of Our Times. V.J. Fontana; The Legal Aspects of Reporting Known and Suspected Child Abuse and Neglect. D.J. Besharov; The Right of an Abused Child to Independent Counsel and the Role of the Child Advocate in Child Abuse Cases. R.J. Redeker, Vill. L. Rev. 23:445-546 (1978).

Negligence-Malpractice-Physician's Liability for Failure to Diagnose and Report Child Abuse. Wayne L. Rev. 23:445-546 (1978).

New Hampshire Juvenile Justice Code of 1969; An

Overview. NHB J. 21:45-88 (1980).

Panel Workshop: Violence, Crime, Sexual Abuse and Addiction (Will, Brigham, Ottenberg, Aytch, Booher, Cox, Cuskey, Del Rio, Densen-Gerber, Francis, Henderson, McLaughlin, Peters, Roether, Sobel, Stokes, Velimesis, Wright) Contemp. Drug 5:385-440 (1976).

Parents' Rights & Juvenile Court Jurisdiction: A Review of Before the Best Interests of the Child. S.Z. Fisher, ABF Res. J. 1981:835-57.

Pennsylvania Child Protective Services Law. Dick. L. Rev. 81:823-36 (1977).

Physical Abuse of Children by Parents: The Criminalization Decision. M.P. Rosenthal, Am. J. Crim. L. 7:41-69 (1979).

Physicians and Surgeons-Infants- Physician's Liability for Noncompliance with Child Abuse Reporting Statute. ND L. Rev. 52:738-44 (1976).

Pragmatic Alternative to Current Legislative Approaches to Child Abuse. B.G. Fraser, Am Crim. L. Rev. 12:103-24 (1974).

Preying on Playgrounds: The Sexploitation of Children in Pornography and Prostitution. Pepperdine L. Rev. 5:809-46 (1978).

Preventing Younth Crime by Preventing Child Neglect. N. Dembits, ABA J. 65:920-2 (1979).

Protection of Children from Use in Pornography: Toward Constitutional & Enforceable Legislation. U. Mich. J.L. Ref. 12:295-337 (1979).

Protecting the Abused and Neglected Child. M.R. Chamberlain. NHB J. 19:25-55 (1977).

Reappraisal of New York's Child Abuse Law: How Far Have We Come? Colum. J.L. & Soc. Prob.13: 91-136 (1977).

Recent Amendments to the Texas Child Abuse Statutes.
St. Mary L.J. 11:914-45 (1980).

Recognition and Protection of the family's Interests
in Child Abuse Proceedings. J. Family L. 13:803-
13 (1973-74).

Recommendation for Court-appointed Counsel in
Child Abuse Proceedings. Miss. L.J. 46:1072-
95 (1975).

Reporting Child Abuse: A Review of the Literature.
A. Sussman. Family L. Q. 8:245-313 (1974).

Seventh Wilfred Fullager Memorial Lecture: "The
Battered Baby & the Limits of Law," J.D. McLean,
Mon. L. R. 5:1-15 (1978).

Sims v. The State Dept. of Public Welfare (438
Supp. 1179): Constitutional Limitations on
Child Abuse Legislation. S.T.L. J. 19:491-
500 (1978).

Standards of Care & Protection Proceedings. J.A.
Cowin, Mass. L. Rev. 66:77-9 (1981).

State Intervention on Behalf of "Neglected"
Children: Standards for Removal of Children
from Their Homes, Monitoring the Status of
Parental Rights. M.S. Wald. Stan. L. Rev. 28:
623-706 (1976).

Symposium: Child Abuse: The Problem of Definition.
T.J. Clements: Child Abuse: An Overview. R.H.
Hays; The Neglect and Abuse of Children: The
Physician's Perspective. R.W. ten Bensel: Child
Abuse: The Legal Framework in Nebraska. Dealing
with Child Abuse in a Unified Family Court.
Mandatory Reporting of Child Abuse in Nebraska.
Creighton L. Rev. 8:729-802 (1975).

Synopsis: Standards Relating to Abuse and Neglect.
BU L. Rev. 57:663-9 (1977).

Termination of Parental Rights and the Lesser
Restrictive Alternative Doctrine. Tulsa L.J.
12:528-44 (1977).

Termination of Parental Rights- Suggested Responses
and Reforms. J. Family L. 16:239-64 (1978).

To Prevent the Abuse of the Future. V.J. Fontana,
Trial 10:14-16 (1974).

Torts: Civil Action Against Physician for Failure
to Report Cases of Suspected Child Abuse. Okla.
L. Rev. 30:482-90 (1977).

Torts: The Battered Child- A Doctor's Civil Liability for Failure to Diagnose and Report. Washington L.J. 16:543-51 (1977).

Towards a More Practical Central Registry. B.G.
Fraser, Denver L.J. 51:509-28 (1974).

Unequal & Inadequate Protection Under the Law;
State Child Abuse Statutes. Geo. Wash. L. Rev.
50:243-74.

Washington Child Abuse Statutes. Gonzaga L. Rev.
12:468-91 (1977).

Who Polices Child Abuse and Neglect on Military
Enclaves Over Which the Federal Government
Exercises Exclusive Jurisdiction? NC Central
L.J. 8:261-7 (1977).

APPENDIX A

DEFINITION OF ABUSE: REPORTING LAWS

ALABAMA
ALA. CODE S 26-14-1 (1) (1977)
"ABUSE." Harm or threatened harm to a child's health or welfare. Harm or threatened harm to a child's health or welfare can occur through nonaccidental physical or mental injury, sexual abuse, or attempted sexual abuse.

ALASKA
ALAS. STAT. S 47.17.070 (1) (SUPP. 1980)
(1) "CHILD ABUSE OR NEGLECT" means that physical injury, sexual abuse, or maltreatment of a child under the age of 18 by a person who is responsible for the child's welfare under circumstances which indicate that the child's health or welfare is harmed or threatened. . .

AMERICAN SAMOA
A.S. CODE TIT. 21, CH. 29, S 2901 (2) (P.L. 15-22, FEBRUARY 25, 1977)
. . ."ABUSE" means any physical injury or mental injury inflicted on a child other than by accidental means or an injury which is at variance with the history given of it; health or welfare is harmed or threatened with harm by the acts or omissions of the person responsible for the welfare; (C) "HARM TO A CHILD'S HEALTH OR WELFARE" occurs when the person responsible for the child's welfare: (1) inflicts or allows to be inflicted upon the child physical or mental injury, including injuries sustained as a result of excessive corporal punishment; (2) commits or allows to be committed against the child a sexual offense as defined in the criminal and correctional code; (3) fails to supply the child with adequate food, clothing, shelter, education or health care though financially able to do so or if offered financial or other reasonable means to do so; "ADEQUATE HEALTH CARE" includes any medical. . .

ARIZONA
ARIZ. REV. STAT. S 8-546 (A) (2) (1974)
. . ."ABUSE" means the infliction of physical or mental injury or the causing of deterioration of a child and shall include failing to maintain reasonable care and treatment or exploiting or overworking a child to such an extent that his health, morals or emotional well-being is endangered.

ARKANSAS
ARK. STAT. ANN. S 42-807 (B) (1977)
. . ."ABUSE" means any physical injury, mental injury, or sexual mistreatment inflicted on a child other than by accidental means, or an injury which is at variance with the history given of it. . .

CALIFORNIA
CAL. PENAL CODE S 11165 (G) (WEST 1980)
(G) "CHILD ABUSE" means a physical injury which is inflicted by other than accidental means on a child by another person. "CHILD ABUSE" also means the sexual assault of a child or any act or omission proscribed by section 273A (willful cruelty or unjustifiable punishment of a child) or 273D (corporal punishment or injury). "CHILD ABUSE" also means the neglect of a child or abuse in out-of-home care, as defined in this article.

FLORIDA
FLA. STAT. ANN. S 827.07 (2) (B) (1981)
. . ."CHILD ABUSE. . ." means harm or threatened harm to a child's physical or mental health or welfare by the acts or omissions of the parent or other person responsible for the child's welfare.

GUAM
GUAM GOV'T CODE S 9120.20(B),(C),(D),(F),(G), 1978 P.L. 14-137, 14th LEGISLATURE

(B) "ABUSED OR NEGLECTED CHILD" means a child whose physical or mental health or welfare is harmed or threatened with harm by the acts or omissions of the person responsible for the welfare; (C) "HARM" to a child's health or welfare occurs when the person responsible for the child's welfare: (1) inflicts or allows to be inflicted upon the child physical or mental injury, including injuries sustained as a result of excessive corporal punishment; (2) commits or allows to be committed against the child a sexual offense as defined in the criminal and correctional code; (3) fails to supply the child with adequate food, clothing, shelter, education or health care though financially able to do so or if offered financial or other reasonable means to do so; "ADEQUATE HEALTH CARE" includes any medical or non-medical health care permitted or authorized under territorial law; (4) abandons the child; or (5) fails to provide the child with adequate care, supervision or guardianship by specific acts or omissions of a similarly serious nature requiring the intervention of the child protective service or a court. . .(D) "THREATENED HARM" means a substantial risk of harm; (F) "PHYSICAL INJURY" means death, disfigurement, or the impairment of any bodily organ; (G) "MENTAL INJURY" means an injury to the intellectual or psychological capacity of a child as evidenced by an observable and substantial impairment in his ability to function within a normal range of performance and behavior with due regard to his culture. . .

HAWAII
HAWAII REV. STAT. S 350-1 (A) (SUPP. 1980)

. . ."ABUSE OR NEGLECT". . . means physical injury, psychological abuse and neglect, sexual abuse, negligent treatment, or maltreatment of a child . . . under circumstances which indicate that the minor's health or welfare has been or is harmed or threatened. . .

IDAHO
IDAHO CODE S 16-1602 (A) (1979)

. . ."ABUSED" means any case in which a child has been the victim of conduct resulting in skin bruising, bleeding, malnutrition, sexual molestation, burns, fracture of any bone, subdural hematoma, soft tissue swelling, failure to thrive or death, and such condition or death is not justifiably explained, or where the history given concerning such condition or death, or the circumstances indicate that such condition or death may not be the product of an accidental occurrence.

ILLINOIS
ILL. ANN. STAT. CH. 23, S 2053 (SMITH-HURD SUPP. 1981) AS AMENDED P.A. 81-1480, 1980 ILL. LEGIS. SERV. 1563

"ABUSED CHILD" means a child whose parent or immediate family member, or any person responsible for the child's welfare, or any individual residing in the same home as the child, or a paramour of the child's parent: A. inflicts, causes to be inflicted, or allows to be inflicted upon such child physical injury, by other than accidental means, which causes death, disfigurement, impairment of physical or emotional health, or loss or impairment of any bodily function; B. creates a substantial risk of physical injury to such child by other than accidental means. . . C. commits or allows to be committed any sex offense listed in the criminal code. . . against any child under 18. D. commits or allows to be committed an act or acts of torture upon such child; or E. inflicts excessive corporal punishment.

128

INDIANA
IND. CODE ANN. S 31-6-11-2 (REPL. VOL. 1980) (BURNS)
"CHILD ABUSE OR NEGLECT" refers to a child who is alleged to be a child in need of services as defined by IC 31-6-4-3 (A)(1) through IC 31-6-4-3 (A)(6)

IOWA
IOWA CODE ANN. S 232.68 (2) (SUPP. 1979)
...Harm or threatened harm occurring through: A. any non-accidental physical injury, or injury which is at variance with the history given of it, suffered by a child as the result of the acts or omissions of a person responsible for the care of the child; B. the commission of any sexual offense with or to a child. . .as a result of the acts or omissions of the person responsible for the care of the child; C. the failure on the part of a person responsible for the care of a child to provide for the adequate food, shelter, clothing or other care necessary for the child's health and welfare when financially able to do so or when offered financial or other reasonable means to do so. . .

KANSAS
KAN. STAT. S 38-722 (A) (SUPP. 1980)
..."PHYSICAL OR MENTAL ABUSE OR NEGLECT" means the infliction of physical or mental injury or the causing of deterioration of a child and shall include failing to maintain reasonable care and treatment, sexual abuse, negligent treatment or maltreatment or exploiting a child to such an extent that the child's health, morals or emotional well-being is endangered. . .

KENTUCKY
KY. REV. STAT. S 199.011 (6) (SUPP. 1980)
..."ABUSED OR NEGLECTED CHILD" means a child whose health or welfare is harmed or threatened with harm when his parent, guardian or other person who has the permanent or temporary care, custody or responsibility for the supervision of the child: inflicts or allows to be inflicted upon the child, physical or mental injury to the child by other than accidental means; creates or allows to be created a risk of physical or mental injury to the child by other than accidental means; commits or allows to be committed an act of sexual abuse upon the child; willfully abandons or exploits such child; does not provide . . . adequate care and supervision, food, clothing and shelter, education, or medical care necessary for the child's well-being. . .

LOUISIANA
LA. REV. STAT. S 14:403 (B) (3) (SUPP. 1981)
"ABUSE" is the infliction, by a person responsible for the child's care, or physical or mental injury or the causing of the deterioration of a child including but not limited to such means as sexual abuse and/or the exploitation or overwork of a child to such an extent that his health, moral, or emotional well-being is endangered.

MAINE
ME. REV. STAT. TIT. 22, S 4002 (1) (SUPP. 1980)
"ABUSE OR NEGLECT" means a threat to a child's health or welfare by physical or mental injury or impairment, sexual abuse or exploitation, deprivation of essential needs or lack of protection from these, by a person responsible for the child.

MARYLAND
MD. CODE ANN. ART. 27, S 35A (B) (7), (8) (SUPP. 1980)
...(7) "ABUSE" shall mean any: (A) physical injury or injuries sustained by a child as a result of cruel or inhumane treatment or as a result of malicious act or acts by any parent, adoptive parent or other person who has the permanent or temporary care or custody or responsibility for supervision of a minor child (B)

any sexual abuse of a child, whether physical injuries are sustained or not. (8) "SEXUAL ABUSE" shall mean any act or acts involving sexual molestation or exploitation, including but not limited to incest, rape, or sexual offense in any degree, sodomy or unnatural or perverted sexual practices on a child by any parent, adoptive parent or other person who has the permanent or temporary care or custody or responsibility for supervision of a minor child.

MICHIGAN
MICH. COMP. LAWS ANN. S 722.622 (B), (SUPP. 1980-1981)
. . ."CHILD ABUSE" means harm or threatened harm to a child's health or welfare by a person responsible for the child's health or welfare which occurs through non-accidental physical or mental injury, sexual abuse, which includes a violation of section 145C of act no. 328 of The Public Acts of 1931, being section 750.145C of the Michigan compiled laws, or maltreatment.

MINNESOTA
MINN. STAT. ANN. S 625.556 (2) (A), (C) (SUPP. 1981)
. . .(A) "SEXUAL ABUSE" means the subjection by the child's parents, guardian, or person responsible for the child's care, to any act which constitutes a violation of sections 609.342, 609.343, 609.344, or 609.345. . . (C) "PHYSI-CAL ABUSE" means: (I) any physical injury inflicted by a parent, guardian or other person responsible for the child's care on a child other than by accidental means; or (II) any physical injury that cannot reasonably be explained by the history of injuries provided by the parent, guardian or other person responsible for the child's care.

MISSISSIPPI
MISS. CODE ANN. S 43-21-105 (M) (SUPP. 1980)
"ABUSED CHILD" means a child whose parent, guardian or custodian or any person responsible for his care or support, whether legally obligated to do so or not, has caused or allowed to be caused upon said child sexual abuse, emotional abuse or nonaccidental physical injury. . .

MISSOURI
MO. REV. STAT. S 210.110 (1) (1) (SUPP. 1981)
1.(1). . ."ABUSE," any physical injury, sexual abuse, or emotional abuse inflicted on a child other than by accidental means by those responsible for his care, custody, and control.

MONTANA
MONT. REV. CODES ANN. S 41-3-102 (2) (3) (1979)
. . . (2) "ABUSED OR NEGLECTED CHILD" means a child whose normal physical or mental health or welfare is harmed or threatened with harm by the acts or omissions of his parent or other person responsible for his welfare. (3) "HARM TO A CHILD'S HEALTH OR WELFARE" means the harm that occurs whenever the parent or other person responsible for the child's welfare: (A) inflicts or allows to be inflicted upon the child physical or mental injury. . . (B) commits or allows to be committed a sexual assault against the child or exploits the child or allows the child to be exploited for sexual purposes. . .

NEBRASKA
NEB. REV. STAT. S 28-710 (3) (SUPP. 1979)
"ABUSE OR NEGLECT" shall mean knowingly, intentionally, or negligently causing or permitting a minor child or an incompetent or disabled person to be: (A) placed in a situation that may endanger his life or physical or mental health; (B) cruelly confined or cruelly punished; (C) deprived of necessary food, clothing, shelter, or care; (D) left unattended in a motor vehicle, if such minor child is six years of age or younger; or (E) sexually abused.

130

NEVADA
NEV. REV. STAT. S. 200.5011 (1979)
. . .1. "CHILD ABUSE AND NEGLECT" means the nonaccidental physical or mental injury, sexual abuse, negligent treatment or maltreatment of a child . . . by a person who is responsible for the child's welfare under circumstances which indicate that the child's health or welfare is harmed or threatened thereby. . . 3. "SEXUAL ABUSE" includes but is not limited to acts upon a child constituting the crimes of: (A) incest. . . (B) the infamous crime against nature. . . (C) lewdness with a child. . . (D) annoyance or molestation of a minor. . . (E) sado-masochist abuse. . . (F) sexual assault (G) statutory sexual seduction. . .

NEW HAMPSHIRE
N.H. REV. STAT. ANN. SS 169-C:3 II. (SUPP. 1979)
"ABUSED CHILD" means any child who has: (A) been sexually molested; or (B) been sexually exploited; or (C) been intentionally physically injured; or (D) been psychologically injured so that said child exhibits symptoms of emotional problems generally recognized to result from consistent mistreatment or neglect; or (E) been physically injured by other than accidental means.

· NEW JERSEY
N.J. STAT. ANN. S 9:6-8.9 (SUPP. 1981)
. . ."ABUSED CHILD" means a child whose parent, guardian, or other person having his custody and control: A. inflicts or allows to be inflicted upon such child physical injury by other than accidental means which causes or creates a substantial risk of death, or serious or protracted disfigurement, or protracted impairment of physical or emotional health or protracted loss or impairment of the function of any bodily organ; B. creates or allows to be created a substantial or ongoing risk of physical injury to such child by other than accidental means which would be likely to cause death or serious or protracted disfigurement, or protracted loss or impairment of the function of any bodily organ; or C. commits or allows to be committed an act of sexual abuse against the child; D. or a child whose physical, mental, or emotional condition has been impaired or is in imminent danger of becoming impaired as the result of the failure of his parent or guardian, or such other person having his custody and control, to exercise a minimum degree of care (1) in supplying the child with adequate food, clothing, shelter, education, medical or surgical care though financially able to do so or though offered financial or other reasonable means to do so, or (2) in providing the child with proper supervision of guardianship, by unreasonably inflicting or allowing to be inflicted harm, or substantial risk thereof, including the infliction of excessive corporal punishment; or by any other act of a similarly serious nature requiring the aid of the court; or E. who has been willfully abandoned by his parent or guardian, or such other person having his custody and control.

NEW MEXICO
N.M. STAT. ANN. S 32-1-3 (L) (REPL. VOL. 1979)
"NEGLECTED CHILD" or "ABUSED CHILD" means a child: (1) who has been abandoned by his parents, guardian or custodian; or (2) who is without proper parental care and control or subsistence, education, medical or other care or control necessary for his well-being because of the faults or habits of his parents, guardian or custodian or their neglect or refusal, when able to do so, to provide them; or (3) whose parents, guardian or custodian is unable to discharge his responsibilities to and for the child because of incarceration, hospitalization or other physical or mental incapacity; or (4) who has been

placed for care or adoption in violation of the law; or (5) who has been physically, emotionally, psychologically or sexually abused by his parent, guardian or custodian; or (6) who has been sexually exploited by his parents, guardian or custodian; or (7) whose parents, guardian or custodian have knowingly, intentionally or negligently: (A) placed the child in a situation that may endanger his life or health; or (B) tortured, cruelly confined or cruelly punished him.

NEW YORK
N.Y. SOC. SERV. LAW S 412 (1), (2) (McKINNEY 1976), AS AMENDED BY S 412 (1) (McKINNEY SUPP. 1981)
(1) "ABUSED CHILD" means a child under eighteen years of age defined as an abused child by the family court act; (2) a "MALTREATED CHILD" includes a child under eighteen years of age: . . .(B) who has had serious physical injury inflicted upon him by other than accidental means.

NORTH DAKOTA
N.D. CENT. CODE S 50-25.1-02 (1) (SUPP. 1979)
"ABUSED CHILD" means an individual under the age of eighteen years who is suffering from serious physical harm or traumatic abuse caused by other than accidental means by a person responsible for the child's health or welfare.

OKLAHOMA
OKLA. STAT. ANN. TIT. 21, S 845 (SUPP. 1981)
. . ."ABUSE AND NEGLECT" . . . means harm or threatened harm to a child's health or welfare by a person responsible for the child's health or welfare. Harm or threatened harm to a child's health or welfare can occur through: nonaccidental physical or mental injury; sexual abuse, as defined by state law; or negligent treatment or maltreatment, including the failure to provide adequate food, clothing or shelter. . .

OREGON
OR. REV. STAT. S 418.740 (1) (REPL. PART 1979)
. . ."ABUSE" means: (A) any physical injury to a child which has been caused by other than accidental means, including any injury which appears to be at variance with the explanation given of the injury. (B) neglect which leads to physical harm. . . (C) sexual molestation.

PENNSYLVANIA
PA. STAT. ANN. TIT. 11, S 2203 (SUPP. 1981)
. . ."ABUSED CHILD" means a child . . .who exhibits evidence of serious physical or mental injury not explained by the available medical history as being accidental, sexual abuse, or serious physical neglect, if the injury, abuse or neglect has been caused by the acts or omissions of the child's parents or by a person responsible for the child's welfare provided, however, no child shall be deemed to be physically or mentally abused . . . solely on the grounds of environmental factors which are beyond the control of the person responsible for the child's welfare such as inadequate housing, furnishings, income, clothing and medical care. . .

RHODE ISLAND
R.I. GEN. LAWS S 40-11-2 (2), (3) (1977)
. . .(2) "ABUSED AND/OR NEGLECTED CHILD" means a child whose physical or mental health or welfare is harmed or threatened with harm when his parent or other person responsible for his welfare (A) inflicts, or allows to be inflicted upon the child physical or mental injury, including excessive corporal punishment; or (B) creates or allows to be created a substantial risk of physical

or mental injury to the child, including excessive corporal punishment; or (C) commits or allows to be committed, against the child, an act of sexual abuse; or (D) fails to supply the child with adequate food, clothing, shelter, or medical care, though financially able to do so or offered financial or other reasonable means to do so; (E) fails to provide the child with a minimum degree of care or proper supervision or guardianship because of his unwillingness or inability to do so by situations or conditions such as, but not limited to, social or psychiatric problems or disorders, mental incompetency, or the use of a drug, drugs, or alcohol to the extent that the parent or other person responsible for the child's welfare loses his ability or is unwilling to properly care for the child; or (F) abandons or deserts the child. (3) "MENTAL INJURY" includes a state of substantially diminished psychological or intellectual functioning in relation to, but not limited to, such factors as: failure to thrive; ability to think or reason; control of aggressive or self-destructive impulses; acting-out or misbehavior, including incorrigibility, ungovernability, or habitual truancy; provided, however, that such injury must be clearly attributable to the unwillingness or inability of the parent or other person responsible for the child's welfare to exercise a minimum degree of care toward the child. . .

SOUTH CAROLINA

S.C. CODE ANN. CH, 10. S 20-10-20 (B), (C), (D), (F), (G) SUPP. 1980)
(B) "ABUSED OR NEGLECTED CHILD" means a child whose physical or mental health or welfare is harmed or threatened with harm, as defined by items (C) and (D) of this section, by the acts or omissions of his parent, guardian or other person responsible for his welfare. (C) "HARM" to a child's health or welfare can occur when the parent, guardian or other person responsible for his welfare: (1) inflicts or allows to be inflicted upon the child physical or mental injury, including injuries sustained as a result of excessive corporal punishment, but excluding corporal punishment or physical discipline which meets each of the following guidelines: (A) the physical aggression must be administered by a parent or person in loco parentis; (B) it must be perpetrated for the sole purpose of restraining or correcting the child; (C) the force or violence of the discipline must be reasonable in manner and moderate in degree; (D) the force and violence of the discipline must not have brought about permanent or lasting damage to the child; (E) the behavior of the parent must not be reckless or grossly negligent; (2) commits or allows to be committed against the child a sexual offense as defined by the laws of this state; (3) fails to supply the child with adequate food, clothing, shelfter, education as required under Article I of Chapter 65 of Title 59, or health care though financially able to do so or offered financial or other reasonable means to do so. For the purpose of this chapter "ADEQUATE HEALTH CARE" includes any medical or nonmedical remedial health care permitted or authorized under state law; (4) abandons the child, as defined by S 20-11-20, Code of Laws of South Carolina, 1976. . . . (D) "THREATENED HARM" means a substantial risk of harm, as defined by item (C). . . . (F) "PHYSICAL INJURY" means death, disfigurement or impairment of any bodily organ. (G) "MENTAL INJURY" means a substantial impairment of the intellectual, psychological or emotional capacity of a child as evidenced by inhumane, or unconscionable acts and conduct. Provided, nothing herein shall be construed as prohibiting a person responsible for a child's welfare from imposing reasonable restrictions deemed necessary by such person for the intellectual, psychological or emotional well-being of the child by any of the following means or methods: (1) restrictions relating to attendance at amusements, concerts, social events or activities, or theaters; . . .

UTAH
UTAH CODE ANN. S 78-3B-2 (1), (2), (4) (SUPP. 1979)
(1) "CHILD ABUSE OR NEGLECT" means causing harm or threatened harm to a child's health or welfare. (2) "HARM OR THREATENED HARM" means damage or threatening damage to the physical or emotional health and welfare of a child through neglect or abuse and includes causing non-accidental physical or mental injury, sexual abuse, sexual exploitation, or repeated negligent treatment or maltreatment. . . . (4) "A PERSON RESPONSI-BLE. . ." means the child's parent, guardian, or other person responsible for the child's care, whether in the same home as the child, a relative's home, a foster care home, or a residential institution.

VERMONT
VT. STAT. ANN. TIT. 13, S 1352 (A) (2) (SUPP. 1980)
. . ."ABUSE" means physical injury or injuries inflicted upon a child by a parent or other person responsible for his care by other than accidental means, or any other treatment, including sexual abuse, which places that child's life, health, development or welfare in jeopardy or which is likely to result in impairment of the child's health.

VIRGIN ISLANDS
V.I. CODE ANN. TIT. 19, S 172 (SUPP. 1979)
. . ."ABUSE" means any physical or mental injury inflicted on a child other than by accidental means, which causes or creates a substantial risk or death, or serious or protracted disfigurement, or protracted impairment of physical or emotional health or protracted loss or impairment of the function of any bodily organ. . .

VIRGINIA
VA. CODE S 63.1-248.2 (A) (REPL. VOL. 1980)
. . . A. "ABUSED OR NEGLECTED CHILD" shall mean any child . . . whose parents or other person responsible for his care: (1) creates or inflicts, threatens to create or inflict, or allows to be created or inflicted upon such child a physical or mental injury by other than accidental means, or creates a substantial risk of death, disfigurement, impairment of bodily or mental functions; . . .

WASHINGTON
WASH. REV. CODE ANN. S 26.44.020 (12) (SUPP. 1981)
. . "CHILD ABUSE OR NEGLECT" shall mean the injury, sexual abuse, or negligent treatment or maltreatment of a child by a person who is legally responsible for the child's welfare under circumstances which indicate that the child's health, welfare and safety is harmed thereby. An abused child is a child who has been subjected to child abuse or neglect as defined herein . . . provided, that this subsection shall not be construed to authorize interference with child-raising practices, including reasonable parental discipline which are not proved to be injurious to the child's health, welfare and safety.

WISCONSIN
WISC. STAT. ANN. S 48.981 (1) (A), (1979)
"ABUSE" means any physical injury inflicted on a child by other than accidental means, or sexual intercourse or sexual conduct under S. 940.225. In this paragraph, "PHYSICAL INJURY" includes but is not limited to severe bruising, lacerations, fractured bones, burns, internal injuries or any injury constituting great bodily harm under S. 939.22(14).

134

(II) "ABUSE" means inflicting or causing physical or mental injury, harm or imminent danger to the physical or mental health or welfare of a child other than by accidental means, including abandonment, excessive or unreasonable corporal punishment, malnutrition or substantial risk thereof by reason of intentional or unintentional neglect, and the commission or allowing the commission of a sexual offense against a child as defined by law: (A) "MENTAL INJURY" means an injury to the psychological capacity or emotional stability of a child as evidenced by an observable or substantial impairment in his ability to function within a normal range of performance and behavior with due regard to his culture; (B) "PHYSICAL INJURY" means death or any harm to a child including but not limited to disfigurement, impairment of any bodily organ, skin bruising, bleeding, burns, fracture of any bone, subdural hematoma or substantial malnutrition; (C) "SUBSTANTIAL RISK" means a strong possibility as contrasted with a remote or insignificant possibility; (D) "IMMINENT DANGER" includes threatened harm and means a statement, overt act, condition or status which represents an immediate and substantial risk of sexual abuse or physical or mental injury.

NO STATUTES ISSUED TO DATE
FOR THE FOLLOWING STATES/TERRITORY:
GEORGIA, MASSACHUSETTS, NORTH CAROLINA, OHIO, PUERTO RICO, SOUTH DAKOTA, TENNESSEE, TEXAS, WEST VIRGINIA

APPENDIX B
LANDEROS V. FLOOD
131 Cal. Rptr. 69, 551 P2d 389 (1976)

Held, that physician and hospital could be held liable for injuries sustained by the child if they negligently failed to diagnose and report battered child syndrome, resulting in thechild's being returned to her parents and receiving further injuries at their hands.

MOSK, Justice.

In this medical malpractice action plaintiff Gita Landeros, a minor, appeals from a judgment of dismissal entered upon an order sustaining general demurrers to her amended complaint. As will appear, we have concluded that the complaint states a cause of action and hence that the judgment must be reversed.

Plaintiff brought the action by her guardian ad litem against A. J. Flood, a physician, and The San Jose Hospitals & Health Center, Inc. (hereinafter called the San Jose Hospital). The amended complaint purports to allege four "causes of action." As we shall explain, the first three of these are actually alternative theories of recovery alleged in support of a single cause of action for compensatory damages for personal injuries caused by defendants' negligence in failing to properly diagnose and treat the condition from which plaintiff was suffering; the fourth "cause of action" merely adds a claim for punitive damages on allegations that defendants' conduct in this respect was wilful and wanton. Defendants filed general demurrers. The court sustained the demurrers as to the first and second "causes of action" with leave to amend, and as to the third and fourth "causes of action" without leave to amend. Plaintiff elected to stand on her complaint as previously amended, and a judgment dismissing the entire action was therefore entered.[1]

The material factual allegations of the amended complaint are as follows. Plaintiff was born on May 14, 1970. On repeated occasions during the first year of her life she was severely beaten by her mother and the latter's common law husband, one Reyes. On April 26, 1971, when plaintiff was 11 months old, her mother took her to the San Jose Hospital for examination, diagnosis, and treatment. The attending physician was defendant Flood, acting on his own behalf and as agent of defendant San Jose Hospital. At the time plaintiff was suffering from a comminuted spiral fracture of the right tibia and fibula, which gave the appearance of having been caused by a twisting force.[2] Plaintiff's mother had no explanation for this injury. Plaintiff also had bruises over her entire back, together with superficial abrasions on other parts of her body. In addition, she had a nondepressed linear fracture of the skull, which was then in the process of healing.[3] Plaintiff demonstrated fear and apprehension when approached. Inasmuch as all plaintiff's injuries gave the appearance of having been intentionally inflicted

---

1. On this appeal plaintiff has expressly abandoned her claim of punitive damages.

2. A comminuted fracture is "a fracture in which the bone is splintered or crushed into numerous pieces." (Webster's New Inter-Nat.Dict. (3d ed. 1961) p. 457.)

by other persons, she exhibited the medical condition known as the battered child syndrome.

It is alleged that proper diagnosis of plaintiff's condition would have included taking X-rays of her entire skeletal structure, and that such procedure would have revealed the fracture of her skull. Defendants negligently failed to take such X-rays, and thereby negligently failed to diagnose her true condition. It is further alleged that proper medical treatment of plaintiff's battered child syndrome would have included reporting her injuries to local law enforcement authorities or juvenile probation department. Such a report would have resulted in an investigation by the concerned agencies, followed by a placement of plaintiff in protective custody until her safety was assured. Defendants negligently failed to make such report.

The complaint avers that as a proximate result of the foregoing negligence plaintiff was released from the San Jose Hospital without proper diagnosis and treatment of her battered child syndrome, and was returned to the custody of her mother and Reyes who resumed physically abusing her until she sustained traumatic blows to her right eye and back, puncture wounds over her left lower leg and across her back, severe bites on her face, and second and third degree burns of her left hand.

On July 1, 1971, plaintiff was again brought in for medical care, but to a different doctor and hospital. Her battered child syndrome was immediately diagnosed and reported to local police and juvenile probation authorities, and she was taken into protective custody. Following hospitalization and surgery she was placed with foster parents, and the latter subsequently undertook proceedings to adopt her. Plaintiff's mother and Reyes fled the state, but were apprehended, returned for trial,

and convicted of the crime of child abuse. (Pen.Code, 273a.)

With respect to damages the complaint alleges that as a proximate result of defendants' negligence plaintiff suffered painful permanent physical injuries and great mental distress, including the probable loss of use or amputation of her left hand.

The second and third "causes of action" are predicated on defendants' failure to comply with three related sections of the Penal Code. Section 11160 provides in relevant part that every hospital to which any person is brought who is suffering from any injuries inflicted "in violation of any penal law of this State" [4] must report that fact immediately, by telephone and in writing, to the local law enforcement authorities. Section 11161 imposes the identical duty on every physician who has under his care any person suffering from any such injuries. Section 11161.5 deals specifically with child abuse, and declares in pertinent part that in any case in which a minor is under a physician's care or is brought to him for diagnosis, examination or treatment, and "it appears to the physician" from observation of the minor that the latter has any physical injuries "which appear to have been inflicted upon him by other than accidental means by any person," he must report that fact by telephone and in writing to the local law enforcement authorities and the juvenile probation department.[5] All three sections require the report to state the name of the victim, if known, together with his whereabouts and the character and extent of his injuries; and a violation of any of the sections is a misdemeanor (§ 11162).

By means of allegations phrased largely in the statutory language plaintiff undertakes to charge defendants with a duty to comply with section 11161.5 (second "cause of action") and sections 11160 and 11161

---

3. A nondepressed linear skull fracture is ordinarily detectable only by X-ray examination.

4. Among such laws, of course, are the statutes penalizing child abuse. (Pen.Code, §§ 273a, 273d.)

138

(third "cause of action"), and avers that they failed to make the reports thus required by law. Her allegations of proximate cause and damages on these counts are essentially identical to those of the first count.

We have found no case directly in point, but the issues may be decided by reference to well settled principles. Succinctly stated, the rules governing our consideration of this appeal are "that a general demurrer admits the truth of all material factual allegations in the complaint [citation]; that the question of plaintiff's ability to prove these allegations, or the possible difficulty in making such proof does not concern the reviewing court [citations]; and that plaintiff need only plead facts showing that he may be entitled to some relief [citation]." (*Alcorn v. Anbro Engineering, Inc.* (1970) 2 Cal.3d 493, 496, 86 Cal.Rptr. 88, 89, 468 P.2d 216, 217; accord, *Selby Realty Co. v. City of San Buenaventura* (1973) 10 Cal.3d 110, 123, 109 Cal.Rptr. 799, 514 P.2d 111; *Gruenberg v. Aetna Ins. Co.* (1973) 9 Cal.3d 566, 572, 108 Cal.Rptr. 480, 510 P.2d 1032.) On the latter point it is clear that "'In this state negligence may be pleaded in general terms, and that is as true of malpractice cases as it is of other types of negligence cases.'" (*Stafford v. Shultz* (1954) 42 Cal.2d 767, 774, 270 P.2d 1, 5, quoting from *Greninger v. Fischer* (1947) 81 Cal.App.2d 549, 552, 184 P.2d 694; accord, *Rannard v. Lockheed Aircraft Corp.* (1945) 26 Cal.2d 149, 154–157, 157 P.2d 1; *Guilliams v. Hollywood Hospital* (1941) 18 Cal.2d 9, 99–103, 114 P.2d 1; *Weinstock v. Eissler* (1964) 224 Cal.App.2d 212, 236, 36 Cal.Rptr. 537.)

[1] The standard of care in malpractice cases is also well known. With unimportant variations in phrasing, we have consistently held that a physician is required to possess and exercise, in both diagnosis and treatment, that reasonable degree of knowledge and skill which is ordinarily possessed and exercised by other members of his profession in similar circumstances. (*Brown v. Colm* (1974) 11 Cal.3d 639, 642–643, 114 Cal.Rptr. 128, 522 P.2d 688; *Bardessono v. Michels* (1970) 3 Cal.3d 780, 788, 91 Cal.Rptr. 760, 478 P. 2d 480; *Lawless v. Calaway* (1944) 24 Cal.2d 81, 86, 147 P.2d 604; *Hesler v. California Hospital Co.* (1918) 178 Cal. 764, 766–767, 174 P. 654.)

The first question presented, accordingly, is whether the foregoing standard of care includes a requirement that the physician know how to diagnose and treat the battered child syndrome.

It appears from the literature that the battered child syndrome was first tentatively identified and reported to the medical profession in the early 1950s. Further surveys and analyses of the syndrome followed, culminating in a landmark article published in 1962 in the Journal of the American Medical Association. (Kempe et al., *The Battered-Child Syndrome* (1962) 181 A.M.A.J. 17.) Since that date numerous additional studies of the condition have been undertaken, and their results and recommendations publicized in the medical journals.[6]

California courts have not been oblivious to this development. In a prosecution for child abuse reviewed in 1971—the same year as the events here in issue—the Court of Appeal held admissible the testimony of a physician identifying the typical elements of the battered child syndrome. (*People v. Jackson* (1971) 18 Cal.App.3d 504, 506, 95

---

5. The statute imposes the same duty on certain other health care professionals, school officials and teachers, child care supervisors, and social workers.

6. A typical article in the field recites case histories of child abuse, points out the distinguishing signs and symptoms of the battered child syndrome, and advises the practicing physician how to detect and treat the condition. For a detailed survey of the medical literature on the topic from its beginning until 1965, see McCoid, *The Battered Child and Other Assaults Upon the Family: Part One* (1965) 50 Minn.L.Rev. 1, 3–19. A selection of the later articles is cited in Grumet, *The Plaintive Plaintiffs: Victims of the Battered Child Syndrome* (1970) 4 Family L.Q. 296, *passim*.

Cal.Rptr. 919.) The court explained that a physician's diagnosis of battered child syndrome essentially means that the victim's injuries were not inflicted by accidental means, and "This conclusion is based upon an extensive study of the subject by medical science." (*Id.* at p. 507, 95 Cal.Rptr. at p. 921.) Citing portions of the literature referred to hereinabove, the court concluded (*ibid.*) that "the diagnosis of the 'battered child syndrome' has become *an accepted medical diagnosis*." (Italics added.) Indeed, the Court of Appeal added that "Trial courts have long recognized the 'battered child syndrome' and it has been accepted as a legally qualified diagnosis on the trial court level for some time . . . ." (*Id.* at pp. 507–508, 95 Cal.Rptr. at p. 921; accord, *People v. Henson* (1973) 33 N.Y.2d 63, 349 N.Y.S.2d 657, 304 N.E.2d 358, 363–364; *State v. Loss* (1973) 295 Minn. 271, 204 N.W.2d 404, 408–409.)

While helpful, the foregoing general history of the battered child syndrome is not conclusive on the precise question in the case at bar. The question is whether a reasonably prudent physician examining this plaintiff in 1971 would have been led to suspect she was a victim of the battered child syndrome from the particular injuries and circumstances presented to him, would have confirmed that diagnosis by ordering X-rays of her entire skeleton, and would have promptly reported his findings to appropriate authorities to prevent a recurrence of the injuries. There are numerous recommendations to follow each of these diagnostic and treatment procedures in the medical literature cited above.[7]

7. For example, the leading article by Kempe et al., *op. cit. supra*, 181 A.M.A.J. 17, states that "A physician needs to have a high initial level of suspicion of the diagnosis of the battered-child syndrome in instances of subdural hematoma, multiple unexplained fractures at different stages of healing, failure to thrive, when soft tissue swelling or skin bruising are present, or in any other situation where the degree and type of injury is at variance with the history given regarding its occurrence . . . ." (*Id.* at p. 20.) Of the different types of fractures exhibited, an arm or leg fracture caused by a twisting force

[2] Despite these published admonitions to the profession, however, neither this nor any other court possesses the specialized knowledge necessary to resolve the issue as a matter of law. We simply do not know whether the views espoused in the literature had been generally adopted in the medical profession by the year 1971, and whether the ordinarily prudent physician was conducting his practice in accordance therewith. The question remains one of fact, to be decided on the basis of expert testimony: "The standard of care against which the acts of a physician are to be measured is a matter peculiarly within the knowledge of experts; it presents the basic issue in a malpractice action and can only be proved by their testimony [citations], unless the conduct required by the particular circumstances is within the common

is particularly significant because "The extremities are the 'handles' for rough handling" of the child by adults. (*Id.* at p. 22.) The article also contains numerous recommendations to conduct a "radiologic examination of the entire skeleton" for the purpose of confirming the diagnosis, explaining that "To the informed physician, the bones tell a story the child is too young or too frightened to tell." (*Id.* at p. 18.) Finally, on the subject of management of the case it is repeatedly emphasized that the physician "should report possible willful trauma to the police department or any special children's protective service that operates in his community" (*id.* at p. 23) in order to forestall further injury to the child: "All too often, despite the apparent cooperativeness of the parents and their apparent desire to have the child with them, the child returns to his home only to be assaulted again and suffer permanent brain damage or death." (*Id.* at p. 24.)

8. Whether the physician would have followed the procedure of reporting plaintiff's injuries to the authorities, however, is not solely a question of good medical practice. The above-cited reporting statutes (Pen.Code, §§ 11160–11161.5) were in force in 1971. They evidence a determination by the Legislature that in the event a physician does diagnose a battered child syndrome, due care includes a duty to report that fact to the authorities. In other words, since the enactment of these statutes a physician who diagnoses a battered child syndrome will not be heard to say that

knowledge of the layman." (Sins v. Owens (1949) 33 Cal.2d 749, 753, 205 P.2d 3, 5; accord, Brown v. Colm (1974) supra, 11 Cal.3d 639, 643, 114 Cal.Rptr. 128, 522 P.2d 688; Cobbs v. Grant (1972) 8 Cal.3d 229, 236-237, 104 Cal.Rptr. 505, 502 P.2d 1; Huffman v. Lindquist (1951) 37 Cal.2d 465, 473, 234 P.2d 34.)

Inasmuch as the "common knowledge" exception to the foregoing rule does not apply on the facts here alleged, the trial court could not properly conclude as a matter of law that defendants' standard of professional care did not include the diagnostic and treatment procedures outlined in the complaint. Plaintiff is therefore entitled to the opportunity to prove by way of expert testimony that in the circumstances of this case a reasonably prudent physician would have followed those procedures.[8]

other members of his profession would not have made such a report. The same is true of each of the persons and entities covered by this legislation. Accordingly, although expert testimony on the issue of a duty to report is admissible, it is not mandatory.

The statute also lays to rest defendant Flood's concern that if he were required to report his findings to the authorities he might be held liable for violation of the physician-patient privilege. (Evid.Code, § 992.) Section 11161.5 specifically exempts the physician from any civil or criminal liability for making a report pursuant to its terms.

Defendants complain that the first "cause of action" is nevertheless fatally defective because it assertedly fails to allege certain specific facts, i. e., that Dr. Flood negligently treated plaintiff's leg fracture, that proper treatment of that fracture or the bruises on plaintiff's back included taking an X-ray of her skull, and that Dr. Flood negligently failed to ask plaintiff's mother for an explanation of the cause of the fracture. None of these allegations is necessary, however, because they are irrelevant to the gist of the complaint. Plaintiff's theory is that in the circumstances of this case the fracture, the bruises, and the lack of an explanation offered by her mother are themselves indicia of the underlying battered child syndrome of which plaintiff was the victim, and it was that condition which defendants negligently failed to diagnose and treat. For the reasons stated, the complaint adequately alleges the facts necessary to support such a theory.

[3] The second principal question in the case is proximate cause. Under the allegations of the complaint it is evident that the continued beating inflicted on plaintiff by her mother and Reyes after she was released from the San Jose Hospital and returned to their custody constituted an "intervening act" that was the immediate cause in fact of the injuries for which she seeks to recover. (Rest.2d Torts, § 441.) It is well settled in this state, however, that an intervening act does not amount to a "superseding cause" relieving the negligent defendant of liability (id., § 440) if it was reasonably foreseeable: "[A]n actor may be liable if his negligence is a substantial factor in causing an injury, and he is not relieved of liability because of the intervening act of a third person if such act was reasonably foreseeable at the time of his negligent conduct." (Vesely v. Sager (1971) 5 Cal.3d 153, 163, 95 Cal.Rptr. 623, 630, 486 P.2d 151, 158, and cases cited.) Moreover, under section 449 of the Restatement Second of Torts that foreseeability may arise directly from the risk created by the original act of negligence: "If the likelihood that a third person may act in a particular manner is the hazard or one of the hazards which makes the actor negligent, such an act whether innocent, negligent, intentionally tortious, or criminal does not prevent the actor from being liable for harm caused thereby." (Italics added.) (See Vesely v. Sager, supra, at p. 164 of 5 Cal.3d, 95 Cal.Rptr. 623, 486 P.2d 151, and cases cited.)

9. See, e. g., Kempe et al., The Battered-Child Syndrome (1962) 181 A.M.A.J. 17, 24, quoted in footnote 7, ante; Boardman, A Project to Rescue Children from Inflicted Injuries (1962) 7 Soc.Work 43, 49 ("Experiences with the repetitive nature of injuries indicate that an adult who has once injured a child is likely to repeat. . . . [T]he child must be considered to be in grave danger unless his environment can be proved to be safe"); Fontana et al., The "Maltreatment Syndrome" in Children (1963) 269 New England J.Med. 1389, 1393 ("over 50 per cent of these children are liable to secondary injuries

[4] As we recently observed with respect to a determination of duty, however, "foreseeability is a question of fact for the jury." (*Weirum v. RKO General, Inc.* (1975) 15 Cal.3d 40, 46, 123 Cal.Rptr. 468, 471, 539 P.2d 36, 39.) The same rule applies when the issue is whether the intervening act of a third person was foreseeable and therefore did not constitute a superseding cause: in such circumstances "The foreseeability of the risk generally frames a question for the trier of fact" (*Weaver v. Bank of America* (1963) 59 Cal.2d 428, 434, 30 Cal.Rptr. 4, 9, 380 P.2d 644, 649; accord, Rest.2d Torts, § 453, com. b).

We cannot say categorically that an ordinarily prudent physician who had correctly diagnosed that plaintiff was a victim of the battered child syndrome would not have foreseen the likelihood of further serious injuries to her if she were returned directly to the custody of her caretakers. On the contrary, it appears from the professional literature that one of the distinguishing characteristics of the battered child syndrome is that the assault on the victim is not an isolated, atypical event but part of an environmental mosaic of repeated beatings and abuse that will not only continue but will become more severe unless there is appropriate medicolegal intervention.[9] If the risk of a resumption of physical abuse is thus a principal reason why a doctor's failure to diagnose and treat the battered child syndrome constitutes negligence, under section 449 of the

or death if appropriate steps are not taken to remove them from their environment"); Friedman, *The Need for Intensive Follow-Up of Abused Children*, in Helping the Battered Child and his Family (Kempe & Helfer eds. 1972) ch. 6, p. 79 ("it would appear from our investigations that the severe permanent damage associated with the 'battered child syndrome' usually does not occur with the initial incident. [Fns. omitted.] Identification of abuse at this time thus offers an opportunity for intervention with the goal of preventing subsequent trauma and irreversible injury to the child").

Restatement the fact that the risk eventuates does not relieve him of responsibility.

Accordingly, the trial court in the case at bar could not properly rule as a matter of law that the defendants' negligence was not the proximate cause of plaintiff's injuries. Plaintiff is entitled to prove by expert testimony that defendants should reasonably have foreseen that her caretakers were likely to resume their physical abuse and inflict further injuries on her if she were returned directly to their custody.[10]

[5] There remain for consideration plaintiff's allegations that defendants violated Penal Code sections 11160, 11161, and 11161.5, summarized hereinabove, requiring doctors and hospitals to report certain injuries to the authorities. As noted at the outset, the complaint separately sets forth these violations as the second and third "causes of action." In fact, plaintiff has only one cause of action because only one of her primary rights has been invaded— her right to be free from bodily harm: "There was one injury and one cause of action. A single tort can be the foundation for but one claim for damages. [Citations.]" (*Panos v. Great Western Packing Co.* (1943) 21 Cal.2d 636, 638–639, 134 P.

10. Again defendant Flood presses only a technical point of pleading, claiming the allegation of proximate cause is fatally defective because the foreseeability of the intervening conduct of plaintiff's mother and Reyes is not specifically set forth. It is asserted that under the case law such an allegation is mandatory if the foreseeability of the intervening act does not clearly appear from the pleaded facts of negligence and injury. (See, e. g., *Frace v. Long Beach, etc., Sch. Dist.* (1943) 58 Cal.App.2d 566, 137 P.2d 60.) As shown above, however, here the occurrence of the intervening act is the precise hazard to which defendants' conduct is alleged to have negligently exposed plaintiff, and the injuries pleaded are those which a reasonably prudent physician would have foreseen as likely to ensue from that negligence. In these circumstances "The allegations of the complaint are sufficient to present the issue" of proximate cause. (*Custodio v. Bauer* (1967) 251 Cal.App.2d 303, 316–317, 59 Cal.Rptr. 463, 472.)

2d 242, 244.) The charged statutory violations constitute simply an alternative legal theory in support of plaintiff's cause of action for personal injuries. Alternative theories of common law negligence and statutory liability may be pleaded in a single count (*Coleman v. City of Oakland* (1930) 110 Cal.App. 715, 721, 295 P. 59) or in separate counts (3 Witkin, Cal.Procedure (2d ed. 1971) Pleading, § 296, p. 1969); or the statutory basis of liability need not be pleaded at all, as the trial court is required to take judicial notice of acts of the Legislature (Evid.Code, § 451, subd. (a)).

[6] Pursuant to our duty to liberally construe pleadings with a view to achieving substantial justice (Code Civ.Proc., § 452), we therefore treat the second and third "causes of action" as alternative counts setting forth plaintiff's theory of statutory liability. The purpose of that theory is manifestly to raise a presumption that by omitting to report plaintiff's injuries to the authorities as required by law, defendants failed to exercise due care—a presumption now codified in Evidence Code section 669.[11] Defendant Flood correctly concedes that the complaint alleges facts showing compliance with the first, third and fourth of the conditions specified

in subdivision (a) of section 669; he reiterates his contention that the allegations of proximate cause are defective, but for the reasons stated above the point is not well taken. It follows that plaintiff is entitled to prove compliance with each of the four statutory conditions for invoking the presumption of lack of due care, shifting to defendants the burden of rebutting that presumption.[12]

[7] Finally, defendants raise two questions of statutory interpretation. They contend that even if plaintiff may rely on Penal Code section 11161.5 in this case, she cannot invoke sections 11160 and 11161 because the latter are "general" statutes which have assertedly been superseded by the former as a "special" statute on the same topic. But such supersession occurs only when the provisions are "inconsistent" (Code Civ.Proc., § 1859), which is not here the case. Sections 11160 and 11161.5 are directed to different classes of persons, and hence are not inconsistent but complimentary. Sections 11161 and 11161.5 on the other hand, are duplicative of each other to the extent that the former deals with physical injuries unlawfully inflicted on minors and the latter deals with the observation of such injuries by a physician. (See generally Note, *The California Legislative Approach to Problems of Willful Child Abuse* (1966) 54 Cal.L.Rev. 1805, 1814–1815.) But inasmuch as the same penalty is provided for a violation of each section (Pen.Code, § 11162), they do not present an irreconcilable conflict requiring one to give way to the other. (Compare *People v. Gilbert* (1969) 1 Cal.3d 475, 479–480, 82 Cal.Rptr. 724, 462 P.2d 580, and cases cited.) There is nothing to prevent the Legislature from imposing a re-

11. Insofar as relevant here, section 669 provides:

"(a) The failure of a person to exercise due care is presumed if:

"(1) He violated a statute, ordinance, or regulation of a public entity:

"(2) The violation proximately caused death or injury to person or property;

"(3) The death or injury resulted from an occurrence of the nature which the statute, ordinance, or regulation was designed to prevent; and

"(4) The person suffering the death or the injury to his person or property was one of the class of persons for whose protection the statute, ordinance, or regulation was adopted.

"(b) This presumption may be rebutted by proof that:

"(1) The person violating the statute, ordinance, or regulation did what might reasonably be expected of a person of ordinary prudence, acting under similar circumstances, who desired to comply with the law; . . ."

12. A number of recent commentators support this theory of liability. (See, e. g., Isaacson, *Child Abuse Reporting Statutes: The Case for Holding Physicians Civilly Liable for Failing to Report* (1975) 12 San Diego L. Rev. 743, 756–762; Ramsey & Lawler, *The Battered Child Syndrome* (1974) 1 Pepperdine L.Rev. 372; Fraser, *A Pragmatic Alternative to Current Legislative Approaches*

porting requirement on physicians in two separate statutes, even if their coverage apparently overlaps.

Defendants next contend that plaintiff can rely on section 11161.5 only if she can prove that Dr. Flood *in fact* observed her various injuries and *in fact* formed the opinion they were caused by other than accidental means and by another person—in other words, that his failure to comply with the reporting requirement of the statute was intentional rather than negligent. We first note that the complaint in effect so alleges, thereby mooting the issue at this pleading stage. For the guidance of the court at the trial, however, we briefly address the point of proof.

[8] The provision of section 11161.5 is ambiguous with respect to the required state of mind of the physician. It has been suggested that for the purposes of a criminal prosecution "the more reasonable interpretation of the statutory language is that no physician can be convicted unless it is shown that it *actually* appeared to him that the injuries were inflicted upon the child." (Italics added.) (Note, *The California Legislative Approach to Problems of Willful Child Abuse* (1966) 54 Cal.L. Rev. 1805, 1814.) We adopt that construction, as it resolves the ambiguity in favor of the offender. (*People v. Ralph* (1944) 24 Cal.2d 575, 581, 150 P.2d 401.) It is also applicable in the present civil action, because the presumption of lack of due care is predicated inter alia upon proof that the defendant "violated a statute" (Evid.Code, § 669, subd. (a)(1)), here section 11161.5. If plaintiff wishes to satisfy that requirement, it will therefore be necessary for her to persuade the trier of fact that defendant Flood actually observed her

injuries and formed the opinion they were intentionally inflicted on her.[13]

The judgment is reversed.

WRIGHT, C. J., and McCOMB, TOBRINER, SULLIVAN, CLARK and RICHARDSON, JJ., concur.

---

to Child Abuse (1974) 12 Am.Crim.L.Rev. 103, 115 & fn. 51; Paulsen, *Child Abuse Reporting Laws: The Shape of the Legislation* (1967) 67 Colum.L.Rev. 1, 34–36; for a published recommendation to the same effect by one of plaintiff's counsel in the case at bar, see Kohlman, *Malpractice Liability for Failing to Report Child Abuse* (1974) 49 State Bar J. 118.)

The case of "Little Mary Ellen," New York, 1874

1. Henry Bergh takes the case to court

New York Times, April 10, 1874

Henry Bergh (1811-1888) was founder (1866) and president of the Society for the Prevention of Cruelty to Animals.

MR. BERGH ENLARGING HIS SPHERE OF USEFULNESS Inhuman Treatment of a Little Waif—Her Treatment—A Mystery To Be Cleared Up

It appears from proceedings had in Supreme Court. . .yesterday, in the case of a child named Mary Ellen, that Mr. Bergh does not confine the humane impulses of his heart to smoothing the pathway of the brute creation toward the grave or elsewhere, but that he embraces within the sphere of his kindly efforts the human species also. On his petition a special warrant was issued by Judge Lawrence, bringing before him yesterday the little girl in question, the object of Mr. Bergh being to have her taken from her present custodians and placed in charge of some person or persons by whom she shall be more kindly treated. In his petition Mr. Bergh states that about six years since Francis and Mary Connolly, residing at No. 315 West Forty-first street, obtained possession of the child from Mr. Kellock, Superintendent of the Department of Charities; that her parents are unknown; that her present custodians have been in the habit of beating her cruelly, the marks of which are now visible on her person; that her punishment was so cruel and frequent as to attract the attention of the residents in the vicinity of the Connolly's dwelling, through whose information of the fact was conveyed to Mr. Bergh; that her custodians had boasted that they had a good fortune for keeping her; that not only was she cruelly beaten, but rigidly confined, and that there was reason to believe that her keepers were about to remove her out of the jurisdiction of the court and beyond the limits of the State.

Upon this petition, Judge Lawrence issued, not an ordinary writ of habeas corpus, but a special warrant, provided for by section 65 of the Habeas Corpus act, whereby the child was at once taken possession of and brought within the control of the court. Under authority of the warrant thus granted, Officer McDougal took the child into custody, and produced her in court yesterday. She is a bright little girl, with features indicating unusual mental capacity, but with a care-worn, stunted and prematurely old look. Her apparent condition of health, as well as her scanty wardrobe, indicated that no change of custody or condition could be much for the worse.

In his statement of the case to the court Mr. Elbridge T. Gerry, who appeared as counsel for Mr. Bergh, said the child's condition had been discovered by a lady who had been on an errand of mercy to a dying woman in the house adjoining, the latter asserting that she could not die happy until she had made the child's treatment known; that his statement had been corroborated by several of the neighbors; that the charitable lady who made the discovery of these facts had gone to several institutions in the vain hope of having them take the child under their care; that as a last resort she applied to Mr. Bergh, who, though the case was not within the scope of the special act to prevent cruelty to

145

animals, recognized it as being clearly within the general laws of humanity, and promptly gave it his attention. It was urged by council that if the child was not committed to the custody of some proper person, she should be placed in some charitable institution: as, if she was to be returned to her present custodians, it would probably result in her being beaten to death.

The Connollys made no appearance in court, and on her examination the child made a statement as follows: My father and mother are both dead. I don't know how old I am. I have no recollection of a time when I did not live with the Connollys. I call Mrs. Connolly mamma. I have never had but one pair of shoes, but I cannot recollect when that was. I have had no shoes or stockings on this Winter. I have never been allowed to go out of the room where the Connollys were, except in the night time, and then only in the yard. I have never had on a particle of flannel. My bed at night has been only a piece of carpet stretched on the floor underneath a window, and I sleep in my little under-garments, with a quilt over me. I am never allowed to play with any children, or to have any company whatever. Mamma (Mrs. Connolly) has been in the habit of whipping and beating me almost every day. She used to whip me with a twisted whip—a raw hide. The whip always left a black and blue mark on my body. I have now the black and blue marks on my head which were made by mamma, and also a cut on the left side of my forehead which was made by a pair of scissors. (Scissors produced in court.) She struck me with the scissors and cut me; I have no recollection of ever being kissed by any one—have never been kissed by mamma. I have never been taken on my mamma's lap and caressed or petted. I never dared to speak to anybody, because if I did I would get whipped. I have never had, to my recollection, any more clothing than I have at present—a calico dress and skirt. I have seen stockings and other clothes in our room, but was not allowed to put them on. Whenever mamma went out I was locked up in the bedroom. I do not know for what I was whipped—mamma never said anything to me when she whipped me. I do not want to go back to live with mamma, because she beats me so. I have no recollection of ever being on the street in my life.

At this point of the investigation, and adjournament was taken until 10 o'clock A.M., today.

In addition to the foregoing testimony, Messrs. Gerry and Ambrose Monell, counsel on behalf of the application, stated in court that further evidence would be produced corroborating the statement of the child as to the cruelty and neglect which she has sustained; also, as to the mysterious visits of parties to the house of the Connollys, which, taken together with the intelligent and rather refined appearance of the child, tends to the conclusion that she is the child of parents of some prominence in society, who, for some reason have abandoned her to her present undeserved fate.

Before adjournment the child was removed into the Judge's private room, where, apart from all parties to the proceedings, she corroborated before Judge Lawrence her statement as herein given. Counsel on behalf of Mr. Bergh, in his statement to the court, desired it to be clearly understood that the latter's action in the case has been prompted by his feelings and duty as a humane citizen; that in no sense has he acted in his official capacity as President of the Society for Prevention of Cruelty to Animals, but is none the less determined to avail himself of such means as the laws place within his power, to prevent the too frequent cruelties practiced on children.

In ordering the adjournment, Judge Lawrence said he would direct a subpoena to issue for the woman who has the child in charge, as, he said, he had no doubt she could disclose the names of one or both of the child's parents, and

146

he desired to be informed on that point before making a final disposition of the child's custody.

---

2. How Mrs. Connolly obtained Mary Ellen Wilson
New York Times, April 11, 1874.

THE MISSION OF HUMANITY
Continuation of the Proceedings Instituted
by Mr. Bergh on Behalf of the Child,
Mary Ellen Wilson

Proceedings in the case of Mary Ellen Wilson, the little girl of eight years, charged to have been cruelly treated by Francis and Mary Connolly, of No. 315 West Forty-first Street, an account of which appeared in The Times of yesterday, were continued yesterday, before Judge Lawrence, in Supreme Court, Chambers. Quite a number of persons, including several ladies, were attracted to the court by the publicity which had been given to the proceedings had on the previous day, all of them evidently deeply sympathizing with the little neglected waif, whose cause had been espoused by Mr. Bergh. Ten o'clock in the morning, to which the hearing had been adjourned, found the little girl, Mr. Bergh and his counsel, Messrs. Elbridge T. Gerry and Ambrose Monell, and Mrs. Connolly, the former custodian of the girl, all present in court. The first witness put upon the stand was Mrs. Connolly, who testified as follows: I was formerly married to Thomas McCormack, and had three children by him, all of whom are dead. After McCormack's death I married Francis Connolly. Before my first husband died he had told me he had three children by another woman, who was alive, but was a good-for-nothing. I went with McCormack to Mr. Kellock, and got out the child, Mary Ellen Wilson, aged one year and six months to Thomas McCormack, butcher, and his wife, Mary, in February, 1866, and whereby they undertook to report once a year the condition of the child to the Commissioners of Charities and Correction. This indenture was indorsed by Commissioner Isaac Bell and Secretary Brown.

Witness continued as follows: I know this was one of my husband's illegitimate children. He selected this one. The mother's name, I suppose, is Wilson, because Mr. Kellock, the Superintendent, had the name down. Mr. Kellock asked no questions about my relation to the child. I told him I wanted this child. My husband never told me where the woman Wilson lived. We got the child out on the 2d of January, without any paper being served or any receipt for the child. This was the only paper we signed, and it was not signed until the 15th of February. Sometimes my husband told me the mother of the child lived down town. I learned from several people who knew my husband that the woman is still alive. I could not tell who they were. They were laborers who came from work with him and stopped there drinking. I have no way of knowing if the woman is still alive, or if she has any relatives. I never received a cent for supporting this child. At the time I took the child we were living at No. 866 Third Avenue, and my husband said the mother left it there, and he would take it out until such time as she called for it. I have instructed the child according to the undertaking in the indenture—that there is a God, and what it is to lie. I have not instructed her in "the art and mystery of housekeeping," because she is too young. She had a flannel petticoat when she came to me, and I gave her no others.

At this point the witness grew somewhat excited at Mr. Gerry, the examining counsel, whom she assumed to be ignorant of the difficulties of bringing up and governing children, and concluded her testimony by an admission that on but two occasions had she complied with the conditions of the indenture requiring her to report once a year to the Commissioners of Charities and Correction the condition of the child.

New York Times, April 14, 1874.

Mr. Geo. Kellock, Superintendent of Outdoor Poor, testified that a child named Mary Ellen Wilson was indentured from the Department of Charities in 1866, being then eighteen months old; that the records show the same to have been left there on the 21st of May, 1864, by a woman named Mary Score, giving her address as No. 235 Mulberry Street, and who swore that until within three weeks of that time she had received $8 per month for the child's support; had no means of knowing who the child's parents were, and nothing was said by either Mr. McCormack and his wife, Mrs. Connolly, at the time, as to any relationship of either of them to the child; the $8 per month had been paid to Mary Score by the parties leaving the child with her, and it was when that payment stopped that she brought the child to his office. Reference was demanded from Mr. and Mrs. McCormack when they took the child, and they gave their family physician, Dr. Laughlin or McLaughlin, whose statement in reference to them was deemed satisfactory, and an order for the delivery of the child was given accordingly; believes he can find Dr. Laughlin, who lived in the vicinity of Twenty-third street and Third avenue. During the past year about 500 children have passed through the department, and witness has no recollection of this one other than the records of his office record. At this point the further hearing was adjourned to Thursday morning next, at 10 o'clock A.M.

3. Mrs. Connolly found guilty of felonious assault
New York Times, April 22, 1874.

MARY ELLEN WILSON
Mrs. Connolly, the Guardian, Found Guilty, and Sentenced One Year's Imprisonment at Hard Labor

Mary Connolly, the discovery of whose inhuman treatment of the little waif, Mary Ellen Wilson, caused such excitement and indignation in the community, was placed on trial before Recorder Hackett yesterday, in the Court of General Sessions. The prisoner, whose appearance is anything but prepossessing, sat immovable during the proceedings, never lifting her eyes from the ground, except when the child was first placed on the stand. Little Mary Ellen, an interesting-looking child, was neatly dressed in the new clothes provided for her by the humane ladies who have taken an interest in her, and has so much improved since her first appearance in the courts as to be scarcely recognized as the cowering, half-naked child rescued by Mr. Bergh's officers. The child was brought into court in charge of Mrs. Webb, the matron at Police Headquarters. Mr. Bergh occupied a seat beside District Attorney Rollins, and took an active part in the proceedings. There were two indictments against the prisoner, one for feloniously assaulting Mary Ellen Wilson with a pair of scissors on the 7th of April, and the other for a series of assaults committed during the years 1873 and 1874. The trial yesterday was on the indictment charging felonious assault.

The little child was put upon the stand, and having been instructed by Recorder Hackett in the nature and responsibility of an oath, was sworn. At

148

first she answered the questions put to her readily, but soon became frightened and gave way to sobs and tears. She was soon reassured, however, by the kind words of Recorder and District Attorney Rollins, and intelligently detailed the story of her ill-treatment. The scar on her forehead when taken from Mrs. Connolly's house, had been inflicted, she said, by her "mamma" with a pair of scissors. Her "mamma" as she called Mrs. Connolly, had been ripping a quilt, which she held, and stuck her with the scissors because she did not like how the quilt was held. The child stated that she had been repeatedly beaten with a long cane by her "mamma" without having done anything wrong. The general cruelty and neglect of Mrs. Connolly were also testified to by the child, as has already been published in the proceedings of the preliminary examinations. Mrs. Webb, Matron at Police Headquarters, Detective McDougall, Alonzo S. Evans, of Mr. Bergh's society, Mrs. Wheeler of St. Luke's Mission, Mrs. Bingham, from whom the prisoner rented apartments, Mrs. States, and Charles Smith, testified to the bruises and filth on the child's body when rescued from Mrs. Connolly's, and to the instances of ill-treatment which had come to their knowledge. After an able argument from District Attorney Rollins and a charge of characteristics clearness from the Recorder, the jury retired, and after twenty minutes deliberation, returned a verdict of guilty of assault and battery.

Recorder Hackett, addressing the prisoner, said that he had no doubt whatever of her guilt. She had been accorded every opportunity to prove her innocence, and the court was fully satisfied that she had been guilty of gross and wanton cruelty. He would have been satisfied if the jury had found her guilty of the higher offense charged. As a punishment to herself, but more as a warning to others, he would sentence her to the extreme penalty of the law—one year in the Penitentiary at hard labor. The prisoner heard her sentence without moving a muscle, and preserved the same hard, cruel expression of countenance displayed by her during the trial, while being conveyed to the Tombs.

A brother of Mrs. Connolly says that the child was legally adopted by the prisoner, who has the legal proofs in her possession, and will seek to gain the custody of the little one at the expiration of her term of punishment.

---

4. Mary Ellen sent to an asylum
New York Times, Dec. 27, 1875

LITTLE MARY ELLEN FINALLY DISPOSED OF

In the matter of the child Mary Ellen Wilson, rescued from Mary Connolly, and whose grandparents were alleged to be residing in London, Judge Lawrence yesterday decided that the relatives not having been found, the child should be sent to "The Sheltering Arms." It was the case of little Mary Ellen which led to the formation of the Society for the Prevention of Cruelty to Children.

New York Society for the Prevention of Cruelty to Children

---

1. The Society is organized, December, 1874
New York Times, Dec. 17, 1874

Elbridge T. Gerry (1837-1927), lawyer and philanthropist, was legal advisor to the American Society for the Prevention of Cruelty to Animals and served as president of the New York Society for the Prevention of Cruelty to Children from 1879 to 1901.

The apprehension and subsequent conviction of the persecutors of little Mary Ellen, some time since, suggested to Mr. Elbridge T. Gerry, the counsel engaged in the prosecution of the case, the necessity for the existence of an organized society for the prevention of similar acts of atrocity. Upon expressing his views among his friends he found plenty of sympathizers with the movement, but no one sufficiently interested to attempt the formation of such a society. About this time he met Mr. John D. Wright, to whom he stated his plan. The latter at once became warmly interested, and undertook the necessary steps toward effecting an organization. Invitations were extended to a large number of prominent citizens interested in the welfare of children to meet at Association Hall on Tuesday afternoon and many promptly responded. Mr. Gerry defined the object of the meeting which, he said, was to organize a society for the prevention of cruelty to children. There were in existence in this City and State, he said, many excellent institutions, some as charitable corps, and others as State reformatories and asylums, for receiving and caring for little children. Among these ought be cited the Children's Aid Society, Society for the Protection of Destitute Children, etc., and in addition each religious denomination had one or more hospitals and similar institutions devoted to the moral and physical culture of helpless children. These societies, however, only assured the care of their inmates after they had been legally placed in their custody. It was not in the province of these excellent institutions to seek out and rescue from the dens and slums of the City the little unfortunates whose lives were rendered miserable by the system of cruelty and abuse which was constantly practiced upon them by the human brutes who happened to possess the custody or control of them; and this was the defect which it was proposed to remedy by the formation of this society. There were plenty of laws existing on the statute books of the State, which provided for all such cases as had been cited but unfortunately no one had heretofore been held responsible for their enforcement. The Police and prosecuting officers were engaged in the prosecution and conviction of offenses of a graver legal character, and, although they were always ready to aid in enforcing the laws when duly called upon to do so, they could not be expected to discover and prosecute those who claimed the right to ill-treat the children over whom they had an apparent legal control. This society proposed to enforce legally, but energetically, the existing laws and to secure the conviction and punishment of every violation of any of those laws. The society would not interfere with the numerous institutions already existing, but would aid them in their work. It did not propose to aid any religious denomination, and would be kept entirely free from any political influences. Its duty toward the children would be discharged when their future custody should be decided by the courts. The counsel for the society volunteers his gratuitous services in the prosecution of cases reported by its officers during the first year. The Secretary will be entitled to a moderate compensation, but no salary will be paid to the remaining officers.

The Secretary will be provided with a book in which all parties who desire to enroll themselves as members may do so at the office of the society, which will be located temporarily in the office of the Society for the Prevention of Cruelty to Animals, No. 100 East Twenty-second Street. The first annual meeting of the society will be held on December 28, 1875.

INDEX